RETIREMENT TRANSITION

RETIREMENT TRANSITION

An Innovation Approach

PATRICIA WEST DOYLE

MILL CITY PRESS

Mill City Press, Inc.
2301 Lucien Way #415
Maitland, FL 32751
407.339.4217
www.millcitypress.net

Printed in the United States of America

ISBN-13: 978-1-54565-637-2

CONTENTS

CHAPTER 1

INTRODUCTION TO A 21ST CENTURY RETIREMENT LIFE

The challenge in my transition into retirement came in dealing with the psychological factors (identity, competence, structure, stability, social connectivity, purpose) that goes into having a daily life rhythm. So much of retirement planning focuses on the financial planning, providing guidance on investment balance, cash flow management, and how much should you save. But very little talks about How-to-Define the hopefully many days after the big day. How do you create your best retirement life versus just allowing it to (magically) happen?

To paraphrase Buick: this is not your father's retirement. The old vision of retiring to the golf course, spending vacation time with the grandkids, and passively sitting around (waiting to die), is an unfortunately persistent perception of the past. When the concept of retirement was created with people retiring at age sixty-five, life expectancy was sixty-five to sixty-seven. Today's retirement years are longer, retirees are often younger and definitely more healthy, and the world is so full of options, it's almost paralyzing with so many choices.

This next stage of life is no longer about frailty and decline; it is a vibrant and productive stage of life. But, what's right for me? What should I do next? What does twenty to thirty years of a 21st Century Retirement Lifestyle look like for me?

What is "RETIREMENT" today?

In the various books I've been reading, there is a lot of discussion on what to call this next stage of life, and many do not like the term "retirement." This is especially true for early retirees who don't fit the old stereotype perception of old, frail, waiting to die, retiree. I've heard: "I hate having to check the box retired on a document/survey," "You are too young to retire" and "I'm not allowed to retire" from my job because I'm not "old enough." If you're no longer working full-time and have the means to support your non-working lifestyle. . . are you retired or not? Merely unemployed? How about gainfully unemployed? ☺

Today's retirement is not the traditional retirement that was created back in the early 1900s as a way of getting older, slower, and more infirm workers out of the factories to allow room for younger workers. The increase in longevity has put off the frail, inactive years of traditional retirement. But it is not just a continuation of the high responsibility years of career and family. There is possibly more productivity desired, but there is also freedom from responsibility and a desire to "give back" that comes with age. Today ages fifty to seventy-five are <u>peak quality years</u>; this is a third stage of life, not a final one.

Creating this next stage of your life requires transitioning from a work (and possibly raising a family) focus to an ideal blend of life activities that reflects the identity you want (who do you want to be – your personal brand identity), supports the values you find important (links to life purpose), and brings you closer to a life of high satisfaction. Moving away from a work-focused persona requires redefining yourself via personal reflection, patience, persistence (hard work), and being open to possibilities. It is time to slow down and listen to the personal needs (physical, emotional, psychological) that might have been ignored.

The Merrill Lynch/Age Wave Retirement Study in 2016 indicated that people in their retirement years now spend on average 7.5 hours per day in leisure activities. While 92 % agreed that retirement gives greater freedom and flexibility, recent retirees found it challenging to adjust from a work-centered identity. Some (35%) found it hard to structure their own time without work defining it. Others (47%) felt guilty about their leisure activities not being productive.

Where are 21st century retirees spending their leisure time? While statistics are merely averages and should not define your plan, the Merrill Lynch/Age Wave Retirement Study in 2016 indicates that those who are fifty-plus are spending their time staying healthy (83%), relaxing (72%), making family connections (58%), having fun (57%), connecting socially (56%), in personal growth (47%), in spiritual growth (43%), contributing/volunteering (41%), and spending time on entertainment activities (37%). What might these options mean for you?

Does your retirement include working? That is not an oxymoron. Many retirees work part-time to meet certain needs. Some begin second careers in an area that they always wanted to try, including starting a business or going back to school. But I know of some retirees who claimed to "fail at retirement" and returned to work full-time. While in some cases these individuals discovered that they get a lot of personal satisfaction from their work, others, in fact, failed to replace full-time work with anything, and therefore defaulted to go back to work. And in some cases, that work is not fulfilling, but just something to fill the days.

There are so many options today. You can relocate to the beach (or to the mountains or another country), or you can downsize locally, or stay put in your own home. You can take up golf or another hobby you've always wanted to try or improve at. You can find your inner artist, or write a book. You can work or not work. You can volunteer or travel or stay at home. There is no single path to a fulfilling 21st Century Retirement Lifestyle.

Looking at what I did, I realized I have not only crafted an initial new retirement lifestyle, but I also used a clear "How-To Process" for getting there. <u>I applied the Innovation Process I had used for years to create my own 21st Century Retirement Lifestyle</u>. I developed and synthesized (through search and reapply) tools to help me envision my future and decide what to do when I got up in the morning. As a living-through-it real retiree, I know how it feels to have days of low energy and life-happens surprises. I also know that it's possible to build a life that's purposeful, enjoyable, and grounded in our own choices.

This book provides easy-to-use ways to figure out how to spend time on the things that matter to you. Through discussion, questions, worksheets, and personal examples, you will discover ways to:

o   Uncover your own personal meaning and values
o   Identify your personal goals and directions
o   Create healthful habits
o   Plan balanced days and weeks
o   Identify interests for your leisure time
o   Build both consistency and flexibility into your daily life.

Learning Moment: Planning Beyond the Money

My retirement was highly anticipated and poorly prepared. I had done due diligence on the financial side of things, but I had just vague assumptions about what life would be like if I didn't have to work every day. The finances were going to be fine, but I was too busy working to figure out what I was retiring TO! And I'm sure I'm not alone in this regard.

Days after retirement, everything I knew about daily living was gone. Yes, no more pre-dawn alarm clocks; no more endless, mind-numbing meetings; and no more office politics. But also no more regular connections with stimulating conversation and no more feeling of accomplishment for hitting project milestones.

I did not have a plan for being socially connected when 80% of my social connections disappeared because they were work-affiliated.

I did not have a solid plan on getting physically fit, having no pre-retirement fitness/exercise program. And everything you read (and know to be true) is about 'move it or lose it.'

I did not even have a plan for staying mentally sharp, although everyone assumed I would simply keep working doing consulting in my field.

Post-work life did not just happen. I had to "do the work" to create a new life plan - because I was an expert on how to work, but I wasn't very sure about how to live a life. Figuring out what I wanted my daily, weekly, monthly and yearly life to be took time.

I had to learn relationship-building skills to form a new village of connections – from casual conversations to extended-family support.

I needed to create <u>new habits for exercise and movement</u> – things to get me off the couch every day.

I had to learn that it's less about what I want to do (having a plethora of activities booked) and more about who I want to be (understanding what's truly important to me).

I learned that my 21st Century Retirement Lifestyle is whatever I want it to be. Everyone's is different, and figuring out what is truly important to you, and not based on someone else's "should" or assumptions, takes time and self-discovery. Mine took visioning, planning, and then refining the vision and the plan. And time.

Learning about myself, creating new habits, building relationships – all takes time.

Whatever retirement means to you. . .

- Traveling the world as always imagined, unencumbered
- Finally being able to do "that thing" I've always wanted – start new career, focus on a hobby
- Spending time on volunteer work and giving back
- Better balance between work (part-time) and leisure activities
- More time with family (grandkids, extended family)
- Never working again - exploring anything I want to in the world around me. . . full-time leisure and fun
- Doing everything I've always dreamt of and put off – check off that bucket list item by item
- Moving to . . . Maine, Florida, Arizona, Costa Rica, closer to my parents/kids
- What retirement. . . I will continue to work full-time; I'm not retiring! That's my right path.

You will create your own new kind of retirement – unique to your values and dreams – active, fulfilling, healthy. Discover your passion areas, connect with others, and take calculated risks towards meaningful goals to achieve your life vision.

The Work of Retirement

Most folks will agree that a successful, fulfilling retirement is:

"Doing what I want, when I want, and with whom I want."

A big part of the retirement transition is to figure out what all those wants are. What many fail to realize is, figuring out what makes a fulfilling retirement for you takes work – time and effort.

- o Understanding your core values, strengths, and interests takes intense self-knowledge.
- o Knowing what you want to do versus what you should do takes self-reflection.
- o Working through your grief over things lost from your working life, identifying self-limiting beliefs, and unlearning bad habits takes time and effort.
- o Knowing whom you want to spend time with and where you want to spend that time takes contemplation (and possibly conversation with a significant other).

No one else can figure this out for you. Nobody else's plan will be right for you. There is no perfect list of "Five Things To Do" for a happy, satisfying retirement. You have to do the work – the self-reflection, the identification of your future dream path, the sorting of choices, the activation of your dream.

This book is designed to help you do the work. But you need to take the time for introspection. Do the soul-searching. Create the life vision. Be persistent.

SPEND THE TIME - DO THE WORK!

You have to take the responsibility to do the work because your retirement path will be uniquely yours. What will fulfill you? How will you spend your days? Who do you want to spend time with? Where will you be – should I/we move? Do you want to work part-time? How do I find replacements for things I thought I would do, but now physically can't?

And if you're married, what do you both want? How will you balance time together versus time apart? What is the me/you/we plan?

A pet peeve for me has always been the total focus on why something is important. Training classes at work would focus on why something was important, but not tell you how to actually do it. Even now, so much self-help writing focuses on the why. . . why you should have a purpose in life. Why you should live a healthy lifestyle. Why you need to be resilient, practice gratitude, have a strong network of friends. It's often backed up with solid research; I'm not debating these things are important!

This book outlines the how-to process I created as I synthesized my way through many books and talks. Many books on retirement talked about the importance of various aspects of creating a new life, but few gave details on the specific HOW to do it step-by-step.

Often I will add insight from my own personal innovation journey, sharing real-life examples of using the tools, my emotions and learning moments along the journey, and the outputs I ended up with.

This is a HOW-TO process to create a plan for this next, hopefully quite long, life stage. Why a plan? One of my favorite quotes about the importance of a plan is a Japanese proverb:

> *"Vision without action is a daydream.*
> *Action without vision is a nightmare."*

So my process builds from the idea of creating a vision to taking action – action that involves everyday life activities.

This is NOT about the finances in retirement. This is about all the other non-financial stuff - the identity I want (Who do I want to be when I grow up?), the activities I want (heavy on the life, light on the work), and how am I going to accomplish it (goal setting, new habit formation).

This book is about consciously creating the life you want by getting clarity on who you really are, who you want to be, what you want to do, and where you want to go.

What is my advice to soon-to-be retirees?

Do some pre-planning beyond the finances. Think about what is important to you and how you will replace aspects of work life, not the endless meetings or office politics, but the camaraderie and social connections; the sense of accomplishment, purpose, and identity; and even a structure to your days and weeks that work often provides. What are your assumptions of how you will spend a day, week, and month in retirement?

Even with a plan to ease into retirement life, realize that <u>this is probably one of the biggest changes of your life</u>, so allow the stages of transition to occur. Understand you might need to let go of long-held beliefs or long-standing habits. Understand there is a period of uncertainty when things have ended, and others might not have started when you need to just let it be. Be willing to adjust the plan (pre-plan or post-work plan) as life happens, and you get new learning from real life experiences.

And for those like me, already thrust into retirement with no plan beyond the financials?

Take your time putting a plan together. Do the work of self-discovery. Try things on.

Helpful Hints as you get started

- Start a journal/workbook to keep notes in!
- Do the exercises. Not just read them. . . do them!
- Take your time. Re-loop!
- If part of a couple, consider doing exercises concurrently and sharing along the way.

CHAPTER 2

HOW TO CREATE A 21ST CENTURY RETIREMENT LIFE
AN INNOVATION PROCESS

Applying Innovation Expertise to Personal Innovation

For many years, I worked in R&D doing consumer product and brand innovation. I was an expert in the innovation process, and often led teams through the process to define action plans to reach future business goals. So when I retired, I used these skills on myself, looking at me as the "product." I certainly needed to be re-invented - from a workaholic to a what? I didn't even know how to define this "brand new me."

Why did I look to reapplying an innovation process for myself? When working on a product category or a brand, you spend a lot of time thinking about how to grow the business. The innovation process focuses first on <u>defining the future state</u>: "what is the vision – what will the product or brand BE in five or ten years?" This fits so well with retirement transition – <u>Who do I want to BE in five or ten years?</u>

Innovation visioning starts with understanding what the company needs this product/brand <u>to do/be</u>, what the key <u>strengths</u> the current product/brand has to leverage, and what the <u>future world/environment</u> is going to be like. This is similar to personal values, strengths under-standing, and life-domain exploration.

After the vision is clear, the innovation process is about <u>ideating all the possible things</u> we can do on the product/brand to reach that vision. Then time is spent on converging to the best ideas by <u>assessing the possibilities</u> versus the vision and resources. On a personal basis, this translates to creating a life possibilities list and then assessing the best ideas (those that match values, skills, and interest). Once the lead ideas are chosen, it's time to <u>activate</u> them. Some try-on ideas (similar to R&D <u>prototyping</u>), while other ideas can be moved directly to action. The easy and obvious ideas were often moved immediately to execution even in the work world!

The process is <u>not intended to be completely linear</u>, but to involve re-loops as you work through activities in each phase and learn new things about yourself. I also found it helpful to keep a journal of the outcomes of the activities and tools I used.

A Personal Innovation Process
Envision and Implement Your 21st Century Retirement Lifestyle:

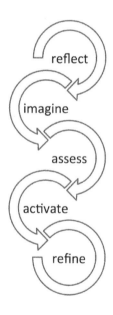

1. **<u>REFLECT</u>**: Self-discovery, know thyself. A deep introspection becomes the foundational insights for creating a "life vision" statement and later providing the basis for assessing activities to be included in an action plan.

> *"Your vision will become clear only*
> *when you can look into your own heart."*
> Carl Jung

Reflecting on who you are and who you want to be so you can decide what stays, what goes, what's added to life so you can live and love the new life you are living. It starts with understanding the identity that is you and not just your work. Doing the deep introspection was helpful, necessary, and took time. Clearly articulated personal values and motivators, skills/strengths, past accomplishments, current and future roles, and interests give the foundational insights to create/build the future vision and plan.

As part of REFELCT, we also will explore a Domains of Life Framework to craft a holistic vision. The framework goes beyond the money to look at multiple elements to consider for your retirement life:

- Location & Lifestyle
- Relationships/Connections
- Self-Development/Generativity
- Health & Wellbeing
- Work/Career
- Hobby/Leisure
- Finances/Prosperity

The framework will be discussed in depth in Chapters 5-9.

Coming out of the REFLECT phase will be a vision statement for your future. And if you have a partner, a joint vision statement as well.

> *"You have to know where you're going before you can get there."*
> John Updike

2. **IMAGINE**: All the possibilities. Creating a "potentials for retirement life" list as output.

This is more than just a task list of "honey-do" projects or a bucket list of all those places to visit (although those things are on it as well). One friend calls his list a "never be bored list."

This phase is creating a list of all future life possibilities, from passions to dreams to inklings - in work, travel, hobbies, volunteering, relationships, lifestyle. It's about skills/talents you want to use and ones to learn or develop. Yes, writing a blog and publishing a book are both on my possibilities list!

A series of brainstorming activities help create a Personal Possibilities List, with hopefully over 150 ideas to finish the IMAGINE phase.

3. **ASSESS**: Compare possibilities to foundational insights and life vision to make choices in creating a Life Portfolio Plan.

It's actually been proven that too many options can cause stress in the selection and in fact lead to lack of choice. Analysis paralysis!

This phase is about choosing activities that best match the vision of life created, which was based on values, strengths, and interests. By making choices, you can focus energy on the important few instead of the insignificant many.

Assessing also helps avoid the busyness for the sake of busyness and have an inner conviction to say "no" to things, even though others will push them as "should." In ASSESS, you chose a *starting* set of activities that fit your vision statement, possibly focusing on a few Life Domains that you defined as more important.

4. **ACTIVATE**: Exploring new activities with setting goals and changing habits. To misquote an often quoted line:

By design or by default, the next life stage will happen.

By making choices and setting goals, you design the life you want to live and the Who you want to be. In ACTIVATE, you set clear goals and measures for each of the specific activities that fit in areas you have chosen in ASSESS. It is also about understanding personal barriers to change and how to break through them. And if you have a partner or spouse, there is the balance of me-time and we-time.

5. <u>**REFINE**</u>: Continual renewals – refresh, rejuvenate, and revise.

Find your rhythm of day-by-day or week-by-week plans that give you a calendar filled with activities that inspire, energize and satisfy. Every couple of months, review your time. If time is flying by and you have plenty of energy, look forward to starting every day, and feel happy and fulfilled - then keep going! If not, adjust: re-look at your Personal Possibilities List for new things to add onto the calendar as others drop off (like completing many of the honey-do projects). If "life happens," then change the plan – pick new Life Domains or even modify the vision statement.

As Thoreau said:

> *"Let go of the past and go for the future.*
> *Go confidently in the direction of your dreams.*
> *Live the life you imagined."*

Things to understand about innovation:

- <u>Innovation takes time and effort</u> - You need time to reflect and to ideate. Time to contemplate and assess. To remember forgotten dreams and envision your legacy. Maybe even some prototyping and reiterating. Defining the future state you want is just as important as identifying what is needed to get there. And sometimes you need to live with the vision a while to see if it "feels right." Pace yourself for the journey.
- <u>Innovation takes courage</u> - Being fearless to try new things, experiment with new skills, push outside the comfort zone. If you're part of a couple, discuss what this means to both of you – the transition, the self-discovery, the future vision – and how there might be conflicting visions.
- <u>Innovation takes creativity</u>. - All the clichés about creativity - think out of the box, play like a kid, think big, think different - do them. And yes, everybody is creative.
- <u>Innovation is fun</u> - Watch for serendipity along the way, look for the open doors, take more shots on goal, and be willing to walk in a different direction if it's not working for you.

Applying innovation practices and process to an individual's life helps guide the individual in designing and delivering an amazing retirement life vision. You and your life become the new invention.

Throughout this book, you will find:

- Cool Tools – How-to approaches and exercises to help you do the self-discovery or assessments.
- Real Life Examples – Example of individuals using the tools, doing the assessments, or answering the questions.
- Learning Moments – My insights, aha's, or reality checks.
- Blog Posts – During my own transition, I began blogging about it. Some of the actual posts are included when they fit the topic being presented. My full blog is at www. retirementtransition.blog

As you work through the process, you will discover and articulate . . .This is who I am today, this is who I want to be, this is what I need to do to be who I want to be, this is how I will do it, here are the choices I make about how I spend my time (an action plan and measures), and this is how I will reward myself when I succeed (rewards along the way).

Things you discover and create along the way can help you in crafting your resume and/or LinkedIn profile, identifying the right volunteering group(s) to engage in, or identifying an entrepreneurial business opportunity - if any of these are in your retirement vision.

However, just like in the real world of innovation, this process is not a check-box activity. There are tools to drive insight – in this case, personal insight. There are tools to help with creating your amazing life vision. There are tools to help create possibilities and work through choices. But they are just tools; you need to do the work – the self-discovery, the choices, the activation. As George Bernard Shaw has said:

"Life isn't about finding yourself.
Life is about creating yourself."

CHAPTER 3

LEARNING TO LET IT BE

As I began moving from full-time, compensated employment to something else, I needed a refresh on <u>how to manage through change</u>.

Retirement is a major life transition, probably one of the biggest in life. As I read through the retirement books and blogs, many discussed how the ending of a career can cause a shock to the system or even be the start of major depression.

Corporate Change Management training acknowledges that transitions have three key phases and <u>transition takes time</u>.

- It takes time to establish a new life rhythm. In the case of retirement, that can mean adjusting to more time in the house, more together time with a spouse, and more alone time. I never realized how much time work took - not only physically getting there and being there, but the mental space that it took as I mulled over issues and problems seemingly 24/7.
- It takes time to sort through and define what could be a passion area. But my nature is a planner, so I need to plan and do, not just think and understand. So it has been a struggle to not just get busy for the sake of being busy - to balance my to-do list nature with allowing time for reflection.

The three phases of transition:

Phase 1 is "let it go." This is time to say goodbye to the past and acknowledge it has ended. Think about work/career and identify what needs were being met that might not be met in the future. What losses will need to be replaced? Think through affiliation, routine, identity and accomplishment. For me, the loss of daily connections to people needed to be replaced, and quickly. Identity was also something I would need to think about. How was I going to answer the infamous question: "What do you do?" without saying: "I'm retired," which says nothing really. Letting it go can also include acknowledging feelings of anger, betrayal or fear, especially if this transition was not as you planned.

Phase 2 is "let it be." Transitions have a period of low energy, a feeling of limbo. You need time to mull over the change occurring. . .time to just "let it be." Think of this time as an incubation period, a fertile time to think and be creative, or the chrysalis that allows the butterfly to emerge. Three of the transition stages in this workbook – Reflect, Imagine, Assess – are about mulling over the transition, taking time to contemplate what comes next, exploring options to discover what might work for you. This phase can often feel like "treading water" rather than moving forward, confusion as to what label to use, frustration in not knowing what's next. Even into the beginning of Activate, this can still be just little steps and not the full-out running into new beginnings. Don't rush through this phase just for the sake of doing something.

Phase 3 is "let it begin." This is a new beginning. This is a state of high energy to start new things, be in new situations, and take on new endeavors. This is moving to action, making commitments to new ways of living, and adopting new habits and activities. And yes, it can be one to two years after your retirement date that you are hitting Phase 3.

BLOG POST: Managing the day-to-day roller coaster

So retirement is all happy, happy, happy, right? Not so much this first year where it felt a little bit like a roller coaster. Many happy, stress-free days but also, the lows did happen. You try something and get negative feedback. You lean in for something and get rejected. You feel totally uncertain doing things when you used to be the expert. You make mistakes. You tell people you are retired, and they look at you as if you said you have a disease. "But what do you do?" You look at your calendar for a full week, and it's completely empty. What do I do?

All these moments have happened to me during this first year of retirement transition. It led me to wonder if I should have retired or just kept working - where I was adding value, connected to others, and appreciated for my expertise. I got stressed. Was I failing at retirement?

So what did I do? I took a deep breath and re-grouped. Okay, maybe it was with a glass of wine and a good friend to whine with. But I took a step back and re-established that I needed to continue to "let it go." In this case, letting go of the expectations of others. Letting go of the need for perfection. Letting go of busy-ness as a sign of worth.

Then I re-looked at my vision statement - the one that states who I want to be in this next life stage. I revisited my choices, my goals, and my action plans. And yes, I was glad I had spent the time on that self-reflection and writing it down! A few times I needed to boost my scheduling of activities - the classes, the walks, the writing time, the coffees and lunch dates. A few times I needed to remind myself that downtime is good - you like to sit in the sun and read books and that is okay on a lazy summer afternoon.

I have also found that it needs to be a balance between a completely filled, to-do based schedule that is over-packed, busy and stressful about missing things, and a whole slew of unstructured, go-with-the-flow, waiting for spontaneity, empty days with nothing to do. So I try to have both - some scheduled time and some unscheduled time.

I saw this phrase recently and loved it: Live a balanced life - learn some and drink some and read some and write some and sing and dance and play and work every day some.

For me, it is learning how to play, or fill the leisure time. For years my husband has said, "We just don't know how to resort" - yes, resort is a verb that defines leisure time. So, I have learned to find joy in the small, leisure things - a fresh cup of coffee on the porch in the morning sunshine, playing Scrabble online, or meeting a friend for happy hour.

I look back on what I have "accomplished" in this first year of transition, which I started without any plan at all. I celebrate the small achievements - my first blog posting, and my second and third ones, too. And the honey-do list completions, with some items that have been on the list for years! I give myself my own gold stars for taking writing classes, computer classes and starting my LLC. I created a "crazy summer fun bucket list". . .and was not disappointed in doing only fourteen of the twenty things - fourteen is better than zero!

And I continue to transition, to find a new rhythm of life. And when the lows happen, I re-group and re-start. And the roller coaster goes back up.

HOW-TO COOL TOOL – Jolts Of Joy

Jolts of Joy is about identifying the little things in life that bring you joy - the small things that just bring a smile to your face, warmth to your heart. Then, once you consciously know what they are, trying to incorporate them into your everyday life.

As a fun activity, consider identifying thirty-one jolts of joy - one for each day of the month. Another creative approach is list twenty-six items from A to Z. This could be an Afternoon Nap to ZZZs in the afternoon! Then, incorporate as many as you can into daily life!

REAL LIFE EXAMPLE: Here is my list of Jolts of Joy (to get you started on your own - because I do believe in stealing and reapplying).

For me, a non-athletic foodie, many had to do with food and relaxation. For you, they could be other things.

1. Bringing order from chaos.
2. Good dinner and good conversation with good friends
3. Afternoon nap in the sun
4. Read a light book - romance, mystery
5. Spend time gardening
6. Nice long walk – in a park with the dog
7. Listen to the rain on the roof, watch the lightning flash
8. Comfortable clothes
9. Open windows, fresh air in the house
10. Farmers' Market
11. Crafts show or artsy galleries/shops
12. Sitting on the porch
13. Get a massage
14. Get a pedicure
15. Eight to nine hours of sleep every night
16. Go to the theater (live theater)
17. Walk on the beach and find shells
18. Holding hands with Tim (that's my hubby)
19. Chopping and sautéing fresh veggies into a stir-fry
20. Craft a new story/concept/idea/model
21. Crisp cotton sheets on the bed
22. Fresh fluffy towels in the bathroom
23. Talking on the phone with my mom
24. Wearing one-of-a-kind jewelry (that people notice)
25. Fresh (summer) tomatoes
26. Fine point blue pens and blank pieces of paper/new journal
27. Fresh pasta dinner with good bread and wine
28. Sushi
29. An awesome piece of chocolate
30. Breaking a sweat doing something healthy - Zumba, hiking
31. Checking things off the list (and making another one)

And yes, I did incorporate quite a few – from buying high-thread-count sheets and a whole bunch of fine-tip blue pens to appreciating the moments I spend doing things I love, like reading, gardening and going to craft shows.

<u>HOW-TO COOL TOOL</u> - **Emotional Monitoring**

Expanded from a concept in ***Ask and It is Given*** by Esther and Jerry Hick, this tool helps identify when your emotions are more negative - discouragement, unworthiness, and doubt. Clearly articulating your real emotion is powerful unto itself. However, you can then think about <u>how you can be more positive. How can you try to move up the emotional scale, even just one or two levels,</u> by practicing gratitude, using positive affirmations, or adding in Jolts of Joy to your day?

Emotions List - Where on the continuum of emotional feelings are you today?

	Emotion
1	Joy, Love
2	Freedom, Empowerment
3	Appreciation, Gratitude
4	Passion, Flow
5	Enthusiasm, Delight, Elated
6	Jubilation, Celebration, Jubilant, Bliss
7	Optimism, Energized
8	Positive Expectation, Hopefulness, Hope
9	Inspired, Eager, Determined, Brave
10	Peacefulness, Serenity, Tranquility, Calm
11	Empathy, Sympathy, Caring, Compassion
12	Contentment, Competent, Able
13	Boredom, Loneliness, Feeling Blah
14	Awaiting, Limbo, Impatience
15	Disconnected, Uneasy
16	Disappointment, Sadness, Discontentment
17	Doubt, Insecurity, Uncertainty
18	Irritation, Frustration, Annoyed, Aggravation

19	Pessimism, Discouraged, Trepidation
20	Overwhelmed, Worry, Anxiety
21	Guilt, Blame
22	Unworthiness, Unwanted, Alienation, Rejected
23	Incompetent, Failure
24	Dejected, Disrespected, Hurt
25	Jealousy, Resentment, Envy
26	Fear, Scared, Battered, Crushed
27	Anger, Hatred, Rage, Revenge
28	Disgust
29	Powerlessness, Helplessness, Disempowerment
30	Depression, Despair

<u>Learning Moment</u> - Choose to be Happy

One of the things I have tried to do during retirement transition is to stay positive about the changes happening. I have to admit, I am more a pessimist by nature, and yes, I definitely have RBF(for those new to that term. . . .resting bitch face).

During my work career, my pessimism showed up in my great critical thinking skills. I could quickly see what might be wrong with a model, a prototype, or an idea and find ways to make it better/stronger. I could think three steps forward and avoid project pitfalls. I always expected the best of myself and of others. I would "tell it like it is," which was usually hard-hitting. Of course, I had a manager who told me I would "never be happy" because I always saw the issues with things. And I've often been told the way to be happier is to just lower my expectations.

So in retirement, I've decided to (try to) be a glass-half-full girl. All the research indicates that being positive is just better – for you and for those around you. One of my seven mantras from day one of retirement was "keep a positive attitude"! Since this is a learning curve, I am using a number of tools regularly to help me do that:

Practice gratitude. I regularly list in my journal what I am grateful for. I made a list of ten for Thanksgiving and then again ten for the New Year.

Jolts of Joy. I've brought many of those elements into my daily life. It's little things – like getting new, fluffy, mint green towels for the bathroom. Every time I step out of the shower, they bring a smile to my face! One woman I met had pink champagne on her list. Now that is her "go-to" drink because, why not?

Emotion Monitoring. I use the language in the list to recognize my emotions daily in my morning journal. And then follow that with how I will choose to be happy, deal with the frustration/anger, and bring joy into my day.

Final Thoughts about Transitioning - Mantras

As I have been working through my retirement transition, a series of mantras have helped me along the journey. I repeatedly go back to these statements when I hit some of the lows or stumble on the path forward.

- **Keep a positive attitude**. This isn't rocket science. Many, many people have successfully navigated the retirement transition. Don't stress the ups and downs of the roller coaster ride. Yes, some days will feel overwhelming, some will feel like you are rudderless, and some will be good ones with feelings of accomplishment. No one embarks on a path not taken before and knows all the challenges, pitfalls, and barriers that lie ahead. But through it all, choose positive, proactive, affirming articulations! I am. I can. I will.

- **Be patient**. This is a major life transition, and transition takes time. As I learned working on the Pantene brand in my previous life, "it won't happen overnight, but it will happen." Take the time needed to deal with the losses you are experiencing and say goodbye to the past - to "let it go." Take the time needed to understand what is important to you, what you need to be satisfied in life. You can't delegate or outsource this work. . . you need to do it and know it. Give yourself permission to relax a bit, allow your body and mind to decompress and find a slower rhythm of life. Take the time to get a good night's rest, exercise regularly, eat well, connect with people, talk it out, enjoy nature, reflect - time to just "let it be." This isn't a race.

- **Know thyself**. Define your Unique Vision. One of life's most difficult things is to truly discover what we really want for ourselves. . . and not just what we've been told to want (the "shoulds") or to do what everybody else does and expects you to also do. It took deep introspection to really understand myself, so I could create the vision of what I wanted my next life stage to look like. Even though I had known me for over fifty years, it took time to really delve into and articulate things in real language and not just MegaCorp speak. I needed to be brutally honest with what I wanted - to be and do - and then work with my significant other to find some common vision elements for creation of the "me/you/we" vision.

- **"Do I really need to work?"** There is a lot of reporting on the Baby Boomer retirement bubble and its potential socio-economic impact. The reality of Social Security and pension/retiree programs with less going in, leaving both the government and private companies under a huge financial drain to maintain the aging Boomers. In the healthy longevity conversation, there are many studies about why keeping both physically and mentally active (which many define as a working life) is so important as we age. So of course, you will work in retirement, every Baby Boomer does. But when it comes down to the INDIVIDUAL, the "yes, you should work" assumptive answer needs to be a bit more detailed. Answer the question for yourself! Do I need to work to generate income (a critical financial reason)? Do I need to work for a psychological or social reason (mental stimulation, social connections), and other activities can provide those needs? What if work takes over life and does not allow time for healthy life activity? What if work is "just a job" and not meaningful or fulfilling? This is another case of know thyself, and not jumping to the "should" expectations of others.

- **Plan for serendipity**. Be open to possibilities. As I thought through knowing myself, creating my vision statement, and thinking about possibilities, the acts of capturing my thoughts by writing things down (journaling, blogging) and then sharing aspects with others were both amazingly helpful. Inspiration came from reading books and blogs and talking to others who are going through the transition or have been through it. You never know where great ideas or connections will come from - they did come and will continue to come.

- **It's OK to NOT be the expert**. I loved being the go-to (expert) person at work. Now I'm a beginner, making mistakes and realizing new habits are hard to form, and new skills take repetition to establish. Does knowing this make it any easier? Not so much. But I am using the tools and skills I have, gathering new ones along the way, asking for guides to help, finding supporters to encourage me, and working to establish new habits. Try it. Explore it. Do it. Yes, it took me twelve months to start my blog. . . . but I did it.

- **Be Not Afraid**. Try it. You will feel the conflict of holding on to the old (comfortable, even if not satisfactory) and moving towards the new (possibly scary, untested waters, maybe even voids). What is the worst thing that could happen if you try something new and it doesn't work out? Everyone says you will regret it so much more if you didn't try it. So what if you fail at it, or are not perfect at it. . . more people will be impressed that you TRIED it!

CHAPTER 4

HAPPINESS BY DESIGN
REFLECT – SELF DISCOVERY

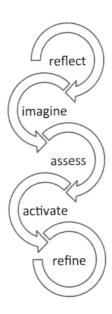

<u>REFLECT</u>

In my exploration of Retirement Transition, I found myself delving into Positive Psychology. Positive Psychology is the science behind happiness. I have always lived under the premise that something will happen by design or by default. You can either design and plan what you want or something else will just happen. Either way, you will live with it. So if I wanted happiness to be part of my future life, I needed to think about designing happiness into my life plan.

Happiness by Design

It was very exciting to me to see that happiness was linked to aspects of self-reflection that were encouraged in retirement transitioning. Happiness theory indicates that when activities we engage in are connected to our interests, they provide a Level 1 kind of happiness - a feeling of pleasure, fun, and enjoyment. These fun activities are secure and comfortable, help us simply enjoy life and spend time with others in pleasurable ways.

When activities we engage in are also connected to our strengths, skills or talents, then they provide a higher degree of happiness, a Level 2 intensity of happiness. Using our strengths in a personally rewarding way creates feelings of engagement, involvement, challenge, and accomplishment and raises the happiness level.

Level 3 happiness is when activities we engage in are also linked to our core underlined values and help us feel part of something bigger. This higher intensity of happiness is often called life meaning, purpose or fulfillment.

This happiness-by-design approach helps in choosing activities and pursuits, but first you need to understand your own values, motivations, strengths, and interests. So we will explore:

- **Values** – understand your core values so you can choose life activities that reflect living them intentionally. What is *most important* to you?
- **Motivators/Needs** – what drives you? Slightly different than values, but very related, this is what you need around you for your values to come to life or what you need to have to be at your best, and satisfied. Understanding your needs and motivations also helps you build what is your personal work style preference? What "floats your boat" or "makes you soar" or "turns you on" (pick your cliché)?
- **Skills/Strengths** – deep understanding of your strengths, skills, competency/ability, and talent/knowledge areas linked with what you like to do can help sort through options on

volunteering activities, part-time work, and/or utilization of strengths in new activities.

- **Interests/Roles** – assess past and possible future interest spaces both in career and in life. What roles do you play today and what roles do you want to play tomorrow? What subjects fascinate you?

REFLECT ON VALUES

At any major transition in life, you want to be conscious of your core values so you can make choices moving forward based on them. The exercises below will help make your core values conscious so you can create your next life stage based on them.

Core values provide the foundation of life. They are linked to what motivates us and what satisfies us. They are unique to each individual and come from an interaction of many factors – from gender, ethnicity and genes to upbringing, education, and religion. They can shift through life as we experience various work, family, social and political environments. Everyone recognizes the same values, but everyone does not necessarily <u>hold</u> the same core values. (And so, the beginning of many conflicts.)

A values assessment is about defining the core values that are held by you . . . . the top five to seven. . . and using the language that works for you. As you look through the list below, pull or craft the language that works for you. . . there is no right or wrong! But really try to get to the top ones – the few that are really important.

There are many, many different values listings in various books – some as long as eighty items. Most psychologists agree that values can be visualized based on two vectors of Risk/Stability and Self/Social. This values universe framework is adapted from ***What Color is Your Parachute in Retirement*** by John E. Nelson and Richard N. Bolles. Some of the "groupings" can get very close. What is important is for you to identify YOUR values with language right for you.

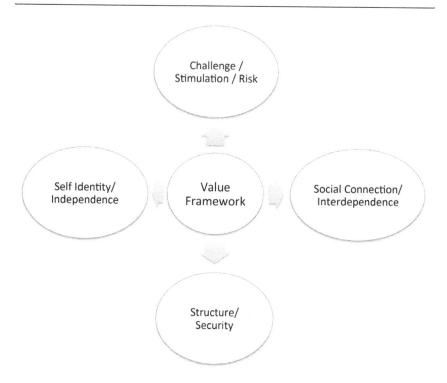

Core Value Area	Other language
Achievement/ Performance	Accomplishment, competition, winning, promotions, ambition, personal success, personal acknowledgment/recognition, visibility, admiration
Connections/ Affiliation	Benevolence, belonging, community, relationships, family, friendships, inclusion, collaboration, caring/nurturing/helping others, loyalty, forgiveness; harmony, balance, teamwork, mentoring
Creativity/ Innovation	Artistry, entrepreneurial, creative media, conceptualization, spontaneity, trends
Expertise/ Mastery	Wisdom, knowledge, mental stimulation, intelligence, logic, competency, intellectual prowess, research, in the "know," authority

Health/ Wellness	Physical stamina, nutrition, inner peace, stress management, personal attractiveness, athletic prowess, physical challenge
Independence/ Self-direction	Freedom, autonomy, individual skill, individuality, personal development/learning, personal creativity, personal choice
Indulgence/ Pleasure	Hedonism, self-indulgence, enjoy life
Organization/ Planning/ Implementation	Structure, productivity, process, output, measures, execution, ethics/standards, follow-through, project completion, decisiveness
Power/Status	Leadership, control, direction setting, dominance, prestige, influence, impact, wealth/ money, prosperity, affluence, material possessions (home, toys)
Security/Stability	Safety, reliability, financial security, routine, certainty, integrity
Traditions/ Religious Beliefs	Humility, modesty, customs, rituals, purpose, personal journey
Stimulation/ Risk-taking	Experimentation, adventure, curiosity, amount/pace of change, pressure, variety, agility, action, adrenaline rush, new experiences, excitement, surprises
Trust/Conformity	Rules, familiarity, respect, respect for elders, comfortable, proper behaviors, Puritan work ethic, politeness
Universalism/ Globalism	Diversity, equality, justice, fairness, world peace, sustainability, commitment to environment, make-a-difference; exposure to cultures, global situations

Some values will be enduring, an innate part of your being. Some might be situational, based on being in this specific life stage. For example, connections became a more important value to me in retirement because I was losing so many of my connections to people as work went away. Financial security went down in importance as I was finally feeling a sense of security with the multitude of reviews I've done on "do we have enough funds."

When considering your true core values, think about when you have manifested these values in action and behaviors. . . .did that feel authentic and satisfying? Often values are pushed on us by external factors – culture, religion, our parents, etc. We feel we "should" value things . . . like diversity, equality, environmental protection, respect for elders, or world peace. But in reality, when the action and behaviors you exhibit are reflective of your core values, you will have a sense of satisfaction. If your actions and behaviors are not reflective of your core values, you will not have a sense of satisfaction.

<u>HOW-TO COOL TOOL</u> – Value Statements

Synthesized from various values tools, this is an exercise to help identify your core values. Consider how each statement comes to life in your behaviors, actions, and activities. Mark X when it really is part of your actions/behaviors/activities, and *when you are doing it, it feels authentic and satisfying*. This is not about what you think you should do/feel, but what feels most authentic.

Where you have an abundance of "x" in a grouping indicates this is one of your core values, and you can then find words in the above chart that best articulate your value.

	Statement	Value area
	I like the feeling of accomplishment when I finish a task or project	Achievement
	Being ambitious and successful is important to me	Achievement
	I love to set and then achieve goals	Achievement
	I feel proud when I use my education, training, experience or skills	Achievement
	I strive to always be better than others	Achievement/ Competition
	I like to participate in activities where there are recognized winners and losers	Achievement/ Competition
	I love the thrill of the game, the art of the deal, the close of the sale	Achievement/ Competition
	I want people to admire what I do	Achievement/ Acknowledgment
	I like it when others publically acknowledge my contributions or talents	Achievement/ Acknowledgment
	I like people to acknowledge me by greeting me by name	Achievement/ Acknowledgment
	It is important for me to be loyal to my friends	Connection
	Forgiving people who have hurt me is an important thing to do	Connection
	I enjoy devoting myself (time, talents) to those close to me	Connection
	I want to leave a legacy for my family, my community, or society	Connection
	It gives me pleasure to help another person grow their skills or knowledge	Connection
	I believe people should follow rules, even when no-one is watching	Conformity/ Rules
	I avoid doing things that people would say are wrong	Conformity/ Rules

	I believe you should always show respect to your parents and other older people	Conformity/ Rules
	It is important to me to obey my parents and/or their teachings	Conformity/
	It is important to be polite to other people all the time	Conformity/
	It is important that I adapt to or fit into situations and not be disruptive	Conformity/
	Thinking up new ideas and being creative is important to me	Creativity
	I love to be part of brainstorming activities - generating new novel ideas	Creativity
	I enjoy tapping into my creative side - with words, visuals, music, art	Creativity
	I look forward to being with people who think differently than I do	Creativity
	I like to be first to see new movies, try a new restaurant, or buy a new hot item	Creativity
	I often do things spontaneously	Creativity
	Staying healthy is very important to me	Health
	I regularly practice meditation	Health
	I enjoy physically challenging myself	Health
	I actively focus on my health - exercise regularly, watch w	Health
	I seek every chance I can to have fu	Indulgence/ Hedonism
	It is important to me to regularly do things just for pleasure	Indulgence/ Hedonism
	I like to "spoil" myself regularly with little luxuries	Indulgence/ Hedonism
	I really want to enjoy life and all the experiences it offers	Indulgence/ Hedonism

	I try to understand all sorts of things	Mastery/Expertise
	I love working with people who are as smart or smarter than me	Mastery/Expertise
	I am curious about many topics and often research, study, take seminars on them	Mastery/Expertise
	I enjoy when people seek me out for my advice or counsel	Mastery/Expertise
	I am happy when projects are completed on time and/or on budget	Organization
	It is important that my things be neat and organized	Organization
	I like to break down problems/activities into manageable tasks	Organization
	I have a weekday and weekend personal routine that I follow	Organization
	I am happiest in a highly organized structure - at work, volunteering, or in a club	Organization
	I get very stressed when things do not go as planned	Organization
	It is important that I be rich (have a lot of money) or own expensive things	Power/Prestig
	I like to tell others what to do	Power/Prestig
	I want to be the one making decisions for the group in most situations	Power/Prestig
	I like to be recognized as the leader of a team, committee, or organization	Power/Prestig
	I like to be able to influence the direction of a team or group	Power/Prestig
	I avoid anything that might endanger my safety	Security
	It is very important to me that my community is a safe place to live	Security
	I actively search for organic or natural foods because I worry about food safety	Security

	I believe the government must be on the watch against threats from outside	Security
	It is important to me to be financially secure in life	Security
	Having a stable government is important to me	Security
	I always like to do things in my own original way	Self-direction
	It is important to me to make my own decisions about what I do	Self-direction
	I like to be free to plan and choose my own activities	Self-direction
	It is important to me to be independent and only rely on myself	Self-direction
	I look for opportunities that will use my unique skills or talents	Self-direction
	It is important to do many different things in life	Stimulation
	I am always looking for new things to try or new adventures to explore	Stimulation
	I like to take risks	Stimulation
	I love surprises	Stimulation
	It is important to be daring and have excitement in my life	Stimulation
	I like to meet different, diverse people and visit different places	Stimulation
	My religious beliefs are very important to me	Tradition/Rituals
	It is best to do things in the traditional ways	Tradition/Rituals
	It is important to me to keep my family customs, traditions and/or rituals	Tradition/Rituals
	I believe in working hard to get ahead in life	Tradition/Rituals
	It is important that every person in the world be treated equally	Universalism

	I believe everyone should have equal opportunities in life	Universalism
	It is important to listen to people who are different than me	Universalism
	I actively do things to look after the environment (like recycle or compost)	Universalism
	I believe all the world's people should live in harmony	Universalism
	I want everyone to be treated fairly and with justice	Universalism
	It is important to protect the weak in society	Universalism
	I am intrigued with multi-cultural issues	Universalism

REFLECT ON MOTIVATIONS/NEEDS

Motivations are elements deep inside you (internally – your brain – heart – ego) that drive your activities (externally – behaviors, things you do) and when matched, provide personal satisfaction. They are different for everyone and reflect what in your unique personality "DNA" needs to be satisfied – in life, a work environment, a volunteer situation, etc.

Motivational drivers can be similar areas to values, but are often more reflected in behaviors and where you spend time that satisfies you. Motivational drivers also might overlap into strengths and skills – think about it as another lens in your self-discovery.

Consider enduring motivational drivers – the things that have been part of your "DNA" for a long, long time. . .whether truly naturally born or nurtured in at an early age. There can also be situational drivers, ones that might shift over time. For me, this was a shift in the hierarchy of financial security not only as a value but also as a driver. . . as I reviewed our financial numbers (for a fifth time) and realized once again we "had enough," I realized that going forward, this would no longer be a driver. However, I am not sure I have totally dealt with the "Do I need a paycheck for the work to be considered accomplishment-grade?" since accomplishment is one of my drivers!

So how do you figure out what motivates you, or identify what are personal drivers? By better articulating your <u>learning and working styles</u> and the "environment" in which you will be motivated to do your best:

- Are you a hands-on creator or more about ideas, the philosophical and theoretical? Do you learn from reading/words or experiencing/things?
- Are you more right- or left-brained?
    o Right is more about creativity, intuition, pictures, relationships, synthesis, and the artistic.
    o Left is more about logic, verbal/words, specific details, analysis, sequential elements, and measurements.
- Are you more about teamwork or individual contribution? Are you more about connecting to others including the reassurance

that comes with that. . . or about being independent with lots of alone time?

- Are you more about being schedule-driven or going free-flow? Do you love competition or not? Do you love a fast paced environment?

- Are you more about "predictable performance" – using talents within comfortable space with low tolerance for mistakes . . . or "innovative learning" - pushing outside your comfort zone with high risk and surprises?

- Are you a. . . .
  o Quick starter – jump right in and learn by trial and error, adjusting along the way
  o Factfinder – compiling and analyzing information, putting together well-formed (i's dotted, and t's crossed) plan
  o Implementer – creating prototypes to see how it looks and feels and modifying
  o Follow-through-er – creating systems and processes (check-lists) to get it done

REFLECT SUMMARY: My Top Five Values are:

- _____
- _____
- _____
- _____
- _____

Additional Insights into My Motivational Drivers/Needs:

- _____
- _____
- _____
- _____
- _____

REFLECT ON SKILLS/STRENGTHS

This section is about better understanding your strengths and skills so you can use them better in the future. Consider what strengths/skills you want to continue to use as you move forward into the next stage of life. Clarifying your strengths and skills helps you select activities that best use them. But, just because you are good at something does not mean you need to keep doing it! Alternatively, are there skills you want to explore and build?

I struggled with the difference between strengths and skills. I like the "strengths are innate, skills are learned" definition:

"Strengths are innate" – almost "what you were born with." These natural talents are not necessarily physicality but could have an aspect of that. They are more preferences, tendencies or dominances that you have. Strengths are usually broad, general and fundamental. You've heard the "he's a natural athlete" (not me!), or she's a "wiz at math" (also not me!) Left-brain (objective, rational, logical) or right-brain (subjective, intuitive, non-linear) thinking, or being an introvert or extrovert, are both commonly used ones.

Conversely, "skills are learned." And many, many skills can be learned! Learning requires repetition, the "10,000 times to become proficient" definition. Skills also tend to be more narrowed and specific. When strengths are combined with skills = true mastery!

There are so many ways to look at this! There are the standard pay-for assessments (from Birkman to StrengthsFinder) to free online assessments to pick lists. As you look through various assessments, look for themes or similarities.

- VIA Signature Strengths (www.viacharacter.org)
- StrengthsFinder (the book/online questionnaire)
- Enneagram Profile (www.enneagraminstitute.com)
- Myers-Briggs - Jung Typology Test™
  (http://www.humanmetrics.com/cgi-win/jtypes2.asp)
- Just ask - Ask those who worked with you "What five words best describe me?"

Whichever you choose (or have already done), you are looking for themes – strengths or skills that come up repeatedly, even if using differnet words.

Some additional possible language for strengths based on innate style and work style preferences is included below. This left-brained/right-brained chart was created based on information in ***The Joy of Retirement*** by David C. Borchard.

	Left Brained – objective, rational, data-based, numbers, science	Right-Brained – subjective, feeling, intuition, relationships, artistry
Cerebral – in the mind	Analytical Thinker – work best with data, facts and abstract concepts, critical thinking, problem-solving, scientific, quantitative, researching, intellectual curiosity, systematizing	Mystical Intuitive – work best with ideas and possibilities, strong imagination, expressive, out-of-box thinking, arts ability (music, dancing, writing, etc.), pattern seeing, envisioning
Interpersonal – with people	Coordinating Organizer – work best with facts/data, policies and procedures; efficient planning, budgeting, inspecting, logistics management; detail focus; high sense of duty; good communications	Nurturing Inspirer – work best with feelings and values; empathetic and empowering; active listening; counseling, influencing, negotiating, consensus building, coaching, mentoring, healing others; facilitating
Kinesthetic – by action	Artisan Craftsperson – works best with hands-on tasks & troubleshooting; technical skills, practicing trade; physicality; individual coordination/dexterity; attention to detail/precision work	Playful Performer – works best with spontaneous action; has stage presence; reactive live-in-the-moment; improvising; composing; hosting; negotiating, moving

Other words <u>if you like to work with data</u>: Synthesizing, innovating, deriving, coordinating, planning, budgeting, analyzing, assessing, interpreting, transcribing, compiling, collating, summarizing, computing

Other words <u>if you like to work with people</u>: mentoring, counseling, negotiating, instructing, teaching, coaching, training, supervising, motivating, persuading, selling, influencing, speaking, serving

Other words <u>if you like to work with things</u>: designing, inventing, prototyping, setting up, restoring, trial runs, building, craftsmanship, operating, problem-solving, driving, machining

In all these reviews, <u>look for themes or similarities. Pick the language that feels best for you</u>. The more you know yourself, the better you can envision/articulate your future. Remember in all this, it is about self-discovery. Be honest with yourself.

<u>REFLECT SUMMARY</u>: My Top Five Strengths/Skills (themes) are:

- _____
- _____
- _____
- _____
- _____

Additional Insights into My Uniqueness:

- _____
- _____
- _____
- _____
- _____

REFLECT ON INTERESTS/ROLES

Roles and interests, descriptors, and "personal branding" all give you crafting language to help define your future vision – the "who" you want to be. It is quite easy to explain your "who" when you are working (or raising kids and coordinating a family). Part of my "who" language for this next life stage needed to be going beyond my "work who" to really explore and create the non-work self I want in the future. In some ways, this was like thinking about work self and non-work self as the left hand and the right hand combined into one complete person.

Being able to express your authentic self is helpful for many reasons. When you can consistently express it in all you do (having it articulated and part of your choices), people will experience you being true to yourself. And, as someone said to me, it gets old very quickly to say you are retired, or an ex-whatever.

This interests and roles exploration helps you say "I am . . . ."! Understanding your interests can also help in future work or volunteering opportunities choices. I recently described an acquaintance with the phrase, "She's an empty-nester mom, an avid athlete who runs and bikes, a great cook, and a doctor, too." (Yeah, can I hate her just a bit?) But that is the litany of role descriptors I strive to create for myself!

Interests and Roles is a bit like going back to the "What do you want to be when you grow up?" thinking and those weird tests you took in high school that said you should be a forest ranger. There are a few tools to help.

Start with basic questions about "What interests me?" "What are my favorite ways to spend time. . . to waste time?"

- What section do I gravitate towards in a bookstore? What magazines do I want to read in the magazine section? Visit a bookstore and wander around!
- What subject would I take a class in if I could? Look at a catalog of courses (The Great Courses or Road Scholar or a local Life-Long Learning Institute).
- What online articles do I double-click on? What websites do I regularly visit?
- What topics do I like to talk to other people about?

49

HOW-TO COOL TOOL – Interest Description List

Interests and other descriptors all give you language of "who" do you want to be? What areas spark interest? What might I want to take a class in? Read a book about?

archeology	culinary arts/food	community services/ development
architecture	engineering/science	design
art/literature	fashion	nutrition/food
astronomy	gaming - online, cards	outdoors/ environment/nature
business management	genealogy	psychology/human development
cars/motorcycles /trains/planes	healing practices	sports
church/religion /mysticism	health care/medical	martial arts
politics	history	stock market/ finances
computers/ websites	law	theater/dance

HOW-TO COOL TOOL – Role Identification

This exercise is a variation on one I found in ***The Joy of Retirement*** by David C. Borchard. You have had many roles in the past that have formed who you are today. And you will have many that define you in the future.

Think about ALL your CURRENT roles, both major and minor. As you move forward, which of your CURRENT roles do you want to keep? Which might you want to expand? Which might be ending? Which do you want to end or reduce? There are things you will be letting go of in this transition, and acknowledging the end of those roles is helpful.

Now, think about your DESIRED roles, any roles you might be interested in to start, to be part of your "who" in the next stage of life, either as a major part or a sometimes part. Blank spaces are to add your own statements!

Prioritize the most important roles moving forward among those you want to KEEP/EXPAND and new roles you DESIRE.

active runner/walker	collaborator	freelancer
Actor	comedian	friend
Adventurer	committee chairperson	fundraiser
Advisor	community activist	gardener/ landscaper
advocate	computer whiz	golf enthusiast/coach
analyst/analytical thinker	concierge	grandparent extraordinaire
animal lover	consensus builder	handyman/ handywoman
animal trainer/handler	consultant	healing practitioner
antique enthusiast/ dealer/collector	coordinator/ organizer	helpmate/ supporter
Artist	craftsman	history enthusiast
assistant/aide	Craft beer brewer	hobbyist
aunt/uncle	culinary cook	homebody/ homemaker
auto racer/car enthusiast	dancer: ballroom, jazz, etc.	horse person/ equestrian
B&B Owner	daughter/son	host/hostess
Big Brother/Big Sister	designer - clothing, interior, home	house renovator
Biker	diplomat	husband/wife
birding/bird watching	director (film/play)	idealist
Blogger	e-Bay enthusiast/ yard sales	implementer
board member	editor	individualist

brand builder	English second language teacher	information synthesizer
brother/sister	entertainer	innovator
business owner	entrepreneur	inspirer
car restorer	executive/director/ president	instigator
card game enthusiast - poker, bridge	family archivist	inventor
Caregiver	fashion designer	investor
carpenter/ woodworker	fashionista	ironman/ ironwoman
cause-oriented activist	film producer	jewelry maker
change agent	financial whiz/ advisor	jokester
Chef	florist	journalist
chessplayer/ champion	flyfisher/fisherman	kite flyer
Christian/Jew/ Muslim/etc.	food connoisseur	planner
club member	foreign language teacher	poet
knitter/quilter	politician	songwriter
Leader	potter	spiritualist
Librarian	problem solver	sports coach
life coach/counselor	product designer	sports enthusiast
Lobbyist	professional association leader	stand-up comedian
Manager	Professional golfer	start-up coach
martial arts expert	professional/career specialist	stepparent
massage therapist	professor	storyteller
matriarch/ patriarch	project leader/manager	teacher

mediator/ negotiator	psychic	tennis player/coach
mentor/coach	public servant	theater lover
mother/father	rancher, cowboy, cowgirl	thinker
mountain climber	reader	tour guide
museum docent	real estate agent/realtor	trainer/fitness coach
music lover	researcher	travel agent
Musician	resort director	tutor
Nurturer	retail store owner	vintner
nutritionist/ dietician	risk taker	volunteer
online gamer	Runner, mara- thon runner	walker/hiker
park ranger	sailor	watercraft lover (boat, kayak, etc.)
party person	salesperson	wedding/ event planner
Peace Corps worker	scholar/ professional student	wine enthusiast/ sommelier/wine maker
personal organizer	Scout leader	world traveler
Pet sitter/walker	screenwriter/play write	Writer
philanthropist	scuba diver	yoga practitioner
philosopher/ theologist	shopper	
physical therapist	social golfer	
pilot	social media whiz	

MY TOP TEN ROLES for the future are:

- _____
- _____
- _____
- _____
- _____
- _____
- _____
- _____
- _____
- _____

<u>HOW-TO COOL TOOL</u> – Accomplishments Assessment

Think back, over a period of years (not just the past few years, go back twenty to twenty-five years!) and list your top ten accomplishments. What ten accomplishments gave me the most satisfaction? What ones would I brag about (do I brag about ☺)? What am I most proud of?

- For each accomplishment, what made it a highlight? Review what kinds of activities/tasks you were doing, the surroundings you were in, who you were doing it with, what skills you were learning, and what strengths you were using.
- After you've detailed each accomplishment, look for themes. . . skills you most enjoyed learning, environments you found most satisfying, etc.
- The things you enjoyed doing → interests!
- The things you felt you did well → strengths, skills!
- The things you were proud of → core values!

If part of your transition includes creating a resume, this is a great dual-purpose activity.

<u>Summary of Interests and Roles</u>

Looking back on all the interests and roles description exercises, what themes have emerged? <u>Again, pick the language that feels best for you.</u> The more you know yourself, the better you can envision/

articulate your future. Remember in all this, it is about self-discovery. Be honest with yourself.

REFLECT SUMMARY: My Top Five Interests/Roles (themes) are:

- _____
- _____
- _____
- _____
- _____

Additional Insights into My Roles:

- _____
- _____
- _____
- _____
- _____
- _____

BRINGING IT ALL TOGETHER

Organizing It for Reference. As you gather all the self-discovery exercises, you are looking <u>for themes, patterns, or repeated ideas</u> - your essential three to five values, your top motivational needs/drivers, your top three to five strengths, your key interest areas, top roles/lifestyle descriptors, and any additional characteristics that you have and/or want to have.

Know thyself. Be honest.

"Essential" Core Values	
Additional Motivational Drivers	
Top Strengths/ Skills	
Key Interests	
Roles/ Lifestyle Preferences	
Additional Language	

CHAPTER 5

VISION BUILDING BLOCKS
REFLECT ON A LIFE DOMAINS
FRAMEWORK

CRAFTING YOUR VISION STATEMENT

The output of the REFLECT phase is vision statement. This goes beyond the vague mental picture of retirement to a strong articulation of the full lifestyle that will energize you (who you will be, where you are going, and what you will do).

The next step is synthesizing all the elements you've learned about yourself to craft this vision – a future that is based on your values, takes full advantage of your talents and strengths, and energizes you because it meets your motivations and needs. This will then be translated into action planning.

Creating a future vision is not easy. Unlocking this inspirational destination can take metaphor elicitation, personal branding exploration, and some life coaching moments. But I do believe, when the destination/vision is clear in your mind and/or written down, serendipity will "take over"!

I found that a Life Domains Framework was helpful in thinking about my future vision. And of course, there are tools and questions for each domain.

Learning Moment - What about PURPOSE?

Many retirement books talk about purpose. They encourage you to find your "greater purpose" in the world, "leave behind your legacy," having something to live for, not just do, or making a difference. And the way to figure this out usually resides in answering the question, "What have you always wanted to do?"

Other words for purpose: life meaning, personal mission, true calling, or your passionate pursuit.

Some people are lucky and know their passion from an early age. They "always wanted to" fly kites, play baseball, make music, write songs. Some find their passion later in life, and by the time they reach retirement transition, they know – I want to be a yoga teacher, make quilts and knit, spend more time volunteering with my animal rescue, make a difference with teens, learn about European history, take care of my grandchildren.

And then there are those like me who struggle. . . what is my passion? What will move my heart and engage my mind so that time just disappears and I am fulfilled? Why don't I know what my purpose in life is?

I finally came to the conclusion: DO NOT WASTE TIME searching for my singular passion, my purpose in life. One might emerge over time, but don't derail now.

It's about finding what really is important to me, and then living it. It doesn't have to be "save the world". . . it can be "make a healthy lifestyle." A "meaningful" life is one that is lived according to one's deeply held values, utilizes one's talents, and leaves this world (whether that is family, friends, workplace or larger community) in a better place from you having been there! But even without an articulated life purpose, getting to the vision statement is what I had to do. . . .the statement of who I wanted to be, what I wanted the future to look like and then writing it down.

A LIFE DOMAINS FRAMEWORK

Through many retirement books and blogs, seven core domains of life were repeatedly discussed as critical elements in creating this next life-stage. Many books about retirement focus heavily on the financial element, but I have found that the six others were as important, if not more important, to think about when creating my new life vision.

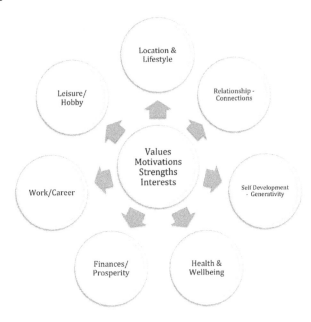

While each domain is explored as a stand-alone, many are inter-connected. Each domain has a whole set of critical questions in the following chapters that can help craft your life vision.

And if you are part of a couple (as I am), comparing answers to these questions can identify areas that need discussion and compromise.

Some of the critical questions of each domain I will explore are captured here:

Finances/Prosperity: Do I/we have a strong awareness of financial plans and money matters – from monthly budget/cash flow to retirement drawdown strategy, including Social Security planning, to insurance needs? Finances are critical to understand everything, from "Do I need supplemental retirement income?" to "Can I travel without worry?" or "Can we afford to buy a second home/condo or fund the toys we want?"

Work/Career: Whether work is needed for income or personal satisfaction, understanding the path forward here is challenging. What is right: career continuation or encore career or bridge job? And then what is the plan to work through job search/new career training if that is the path forward? I also found for me (a Type-A workaholic) that I needed to intentionally limit this domain thinking to allow space for the other domains in my life vision.

Hobby/Leisure: What fun stuff do I/we want to do – from expanding current hobbies to identifying new ones? What fun things will use my strengths/knowledge and/or build new skills? This is a broad topic but it's a great area to make sure is part of your life vision – from learning (your local Life Long Learning Institutes, Roadscholar, or Community College) to travel plans (bucket list destinations) to creative outlets (writing a blog!). What activities in social interaction, spectator appreciation, creative expression, physical exercise, intellectual stimulation, and solitary relaxation?

Relationships/Connections: This domain covers spouse to children to aging parents, other relatives, extended family, and friends. Retirement changes connection dynamics, as you lose touch with work "friends." It can also change family dynamics. Are there unspoken expectations within the extended family for where time will be spent? What connections do I/we need to maintain, improve, build, eliminate? What support networks are there or need to be there (need to be created)?

Health & Wellbeing: This domain includes physical, emotional/mental, spiritual. What is the going forward plan for relaxation (meditation/prayer/spirituality exploration, sleep), nutrition (eating healthy, cooking healthy), activity (physically fit, exercise programs, movement)?

Location & Lifestyle: Choice of location and community can have so many implications – closeness to others, access to work opportunities, support of health and wellness. What lifestyle do we want to live? Are we more interested in rural/connected to nature or urban/close to the hub of activity? What does a home mean to us? Do we downsize, resize, relocate?

Self-Development/Generativity: How do I/we want to share my time, talents and/or treasures? Do I want to focus on local community or a broader cause? What do I want to do to further my self-development? What do I want my legacy to be?

The next chapters will walk through each of these domains.

CHAPTER 6

TO WORK OR NOT TO WORK

WORK/CAREER LIFE DOMAIN

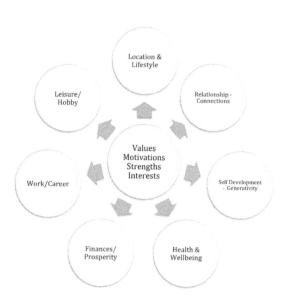

TO WORK OR NOT TO WORK, that is the question, stealing a bit from Shakespeare. But it became a big tension-question as I created my future life vision. There was a HUGE assumption, from one camp, that compensated work would be a given (a "should") in this next stage of my life. It took me a while to understand my answer to the question, "Do I really need to work?"

There is a lot of reporting on the Baby Boomer retirement bubble and its potential socio-economic impact. There is the expected pull out of Social Security and pension programs with less going in, leaving both the government and private companies under a huge financial drain. In the healthy longevity conversation, there are many studies about why keeping both physically and mentally active is important as we age. There is an underlying assumption in many books and articles that because of this increase in longevity, combined with the reduction of pensions and the lack of personal savings, all Baby Boomers will need to have supplemental income in their next stage of life. All Baby Boomers will need to work to provide life meaning/purpose and connection, so they don't shrivel up and die.

Then there was the HUGE assumption from another camp that if you are still working, you're not really retired. Retirement was, simply, not working - a life of leisure and play and volunteering.

When it comes down to the INDIVIDUAL, the question of to work or not to work has both financial and emotional considerations. Yes, there is the "Do you need supplemental income?" in retirement, a critical financial reason. And a good look at your finances and expenses is definitely in order to answer that! [Make sure you have this critical question answered, with the help of a financial planner, if needed.]

But the emotional side of work can be just as important. When you consider what work provided in the past, it is often more than just monetary compensation. What if work was/is the only outlet for fulfilling critical values-based needs? What if your work-style means work takes over life and does not allow for healthy activity? What if work is "just a job" and not meaningful or fulfilling?

Why Work in "Retirement"?

For years, retirement meant the end of your working life. But recently, with increased longevity and earlier retirements (average retirement is now closer to fifty-seven, not sixty-five), a retirement stage of life can easily be twenty-five to thirty years in length. So, many retirees are continuing to work or returning to work. Should you?

Why would someone choose to work in retirement? What needs does/did work provide? Understanding what needs you have moving forward, needs that you are looking for work to provide, can also help you define what that work should look like!

For some, continuing to work really is about the actual financial compensation. With the increased years in retirement, many retirees find that they need the supplemental income that working in their retirement years generates. Sometimes working might also be needed to provide medical benefits in the earlier years of retirement. There is also the element that being monetarily paid for my time is a signal of personal worth. An individual needs to fully understand whether supplemental income (and how much) is a need to be met when looking at working in retirement.

Work provides more than just the financial side; there is the emotional side as well. What did work emotionally provide that is still needed, based on understanding values, needs? In the future is work the only outlet for those needs to be met?

- Did work help provide <u>Sense of Identity and Recognition</u>? Did I introduce myself by saying what work I did? Did I look to work (including perks of the job) or co-workers to build my ego, give me confidence, or provide me status?
- Did work help provide <u>Challenge and Risk and Achievement</u>? Did work provide my (only/primary) mentally stimulating situations/conversations? Did work provide me with the feeling of being "needed" and useful? Was this my only avenue for a feeling of accomplishment?
- Did work help provide <u>Social Affiliation and Friendship</u>? Are most of my friends through work or work-related activities? Did most of my non-work activities evolve around work-related friends?
- Did work help provide <u>Structure and Routine and Time Management</u>? Was work my primary life structure? Do I need structure going forward?

<u>Status and Identity</u> - In your previous life stage, work probably provided you with a significant portion of your Who – your identity, status, and recognition. It gave you a place to fit into social structure and community. For some it provided work perks that will now go away – travel benefits or organizational memberships. How will you create identity in this next life stage? I've spoken to some retirees who had to simultaneously deal with losing work identity and "parent" identity as their adult children left them as empty nesters. Work might be your best solution for filling this "Who Am I?" need, but it's not the only option. Are you looking to work to help provide you with identity?

Achievement and Utility - Again, work life was often the primary source of feelings of achievement and being "needed." It provided everything from problem-solving opportunities to intellectual debates to meeting project milestones. It provided a sense of being in the game. What specifically do you need for continued fulfillment here? Is it the feeling of competition or the completion of goals/projects? Is it recognition of the accomplishment? As stated above, for many, monetary compensation can be a key measure of utility. If achievement is a strong value-based need moving forward, what in your total life portfolio will help fill it? Is working for compensation the best option?

Social Affiliation and Connection - I have pointed out to many that when I stopped working full-time, I lost 80% of my "regular" connections. From the coffee chatter and lunch buddies to group projects and team meetings, even an introvert has a lot of social connection needs being met. My husband just could not fill all my daily people interaction needs. Understanding what your relationship profile looks like entering retirement, and what you want it to look like, could mean work is a critical going-forward solution. By relationship profile I mean: professional relationships, social friends, spouse/significant other, and family. Are you looking for work to provide social interaction and connection?

Time Management and Structure - Working provided structure. Whether we liked it or not, it dictated when to wake up, when to eat, when to run errands, where to be at what time of the day. And while many a retiree will say, "I never want to have a schedule again," people do need to have a sense of a daily schedule and will, whether written or unwritten, have one. Some people need more time management than others. (I need quite a bit.) Working in retirement can help someone craft a self-controlled schedule that makes a total life portfolio flow. Is time management a need that work will provide for you? Or can you find other ways to self-schedule your life?

The "to work or not to work" question requires an individual to:

- Understand his/her own needs
- Analyze if working is the best option to meet those needs,
- And then look for work that meets those specific individual needs.

Retirement requires creating new ways to provide benefits that work provided and might still be needed. You might no longer have the title, the pay, the work perks, the peer feedback that validates your thinking, the daily structure, or the project milestones that indicate accomplishment. Continuing to work can be part of your personal needs. Only once BOTH the financial AND emotional parts of work are understood can you begin to explore what type of work you should you be looking for (if any) in this next life stage.

HOW-TO COOL TOOL – TO WORK OR NOT TO WORK
Benefit Assessment

Below, identify how important each benefit of work is to you (scale 1-5, with 1 being not important to 5 being highly important), how you are meeting it now, and some ideas for how you might meet it in the future. For example, you might rate socialization as very important (4) and recognize that it is not being met outside of work now with limited friendships outside of work colleagues, but you can think about joining a club or doing volunteer work in the future.

Benefit	Importance Rating	How met now?	Ideas: How met in future?
Financial Compensation: Supplemental income and medical benefits; Understanding of cash flow; Money for lifestyle desired			
Status and Identity: Who am I? Need for recognition? What is my place in community?			
Acievement and Utility: Feeling of Accomplishment: Feeling of usefulness; Sense of purpose			
Socialization and Affiliation: Connection and interaction with others			
Time Management and Structure: Daily routines; Goal setting			

Once you are clear on your individual needs, some paths forward to work include:

Career Continuation - You loved your work. You might not have been 100% ready to retire, can't imagine not working in your current profession, and have more to achieve or contribute. As a Career Continuer, you want to capitalize on your work experience and skills. Consider working with a consulting company (like YourEncore), establishing your own consulting practice in your field of expertise, teaching as an adjunct professor, leading a professional association, becoming editor of a journal in your field of expertise, writing and publishing books in your field, creating and selling digital downloads/training, or becoming a speaker/corporate trainer/coach.

Explore an Encore Career - You regret not trying a different work/career opportunity at some point in your life. You have the "if only I had" hindsight. Or maybe you want to use your talents/skills in a new career passion area, or finally start your own business to be your own boss. If this feels like the right space, consider buying into a franchise/licensee program, returning to college for a new degree in something you always wanted, retraining or licensing/certification for a new trade. Consider your areas of interest for a new career: do you love performance (musician, actor, comedian), working with others (mediator, teacher, realtor, minister), or the medical field (healthcare worker/practitioner, massage therapy)?

A Fun Bridge Job - You need some supplemental income, but are not interested in a career-focused area. Or you are considering turning a lifelong hobby/interest into part-time income generation, where you work only as much as you want. There are so many areas that might satisfy this space, especially small business creation for day-to-day needs/services like: dog walker, driver, personal shopper, tax prep, personal concierge/organizer, personal chef, business support services, home stager, proofreader, website developer, or home companion. Or a part-time job in your area of interest/hobby area that brings with it some unique perks - seasonal work (summer camps, national parks, garden store at peak times), retail in passion area (fashion, home improvement, cooking, home décor, sport), or becoming a fitness instructor (yoga, Zumba).

Also to consider if compensation is not needed at all but a work structure could help deliver some work-related needs:

New Adventurers - This is where you don't really need supplemental retirement income. You want to experience new adventures, explore new avenues, or learn new things/skills. You have latent talents/skills/passions you want to expand or new talents/skills you always wanted to develop. You can build on a passionate hobby or master a craft, with possible minimal compensation. To identify new adventure opportunities, consider exploring leagues or local chapters in areas of interest, getting advanced education for the sake of learning (ex. a local Life Long Learning center, Road Scholar). Some out-there ideas with minimal compensation – join the Peace Corps, become a tour director/adventure tour guide, be a professional e-Bay buyer/seller, sell your crafts at shows.

Purposeful Volunteer - If you have a strong desire to give back, consider working at the local hospital/food pantry/school. Become a volunteer at a local art museum, zoo, or historical site. Become a mentor or use your skills with a non-profit.

REAL LIFE EXAMPLE: Yes, I am one of those. I was the workaholic who identified myself by what I did at work and had a limited life outside of work. The one the experts say will struggle most in retirement transition to find out who they are without work.

As I struggled with to work or not to work, I decided to pursue a path I had considered twice in my life but didn't take either time. Yes, the Robert Frost poem comes to mind. . . two paths diverged. Had I kept the path for a later day and now was the time? I've always been happy with taking that path less traveled - the female engineer, a technical (STEM) path, and feminist role model. It fit my practical, rational, critical thinking style.

Becoming a Life Coach felt so female! So touchy-feely. Yet, when I looked into Life Coach with a Retirement Focus, the first two folks I talked to were men. I had all this knowledge having researched in-depth retirement transition and even created a process with associated exercises to move through it. Why not?

How did this all come about?

Contemplating the To Work or Not to Work Benefit Assessment, I realized I needed some work to mentally challenge myself, to help provide an identity, and to provide some income for self-worth. I did not need to work for any financial reasons.

I started with Career Continuation in my mastery area. I still love doing that work, but it was specialized to the MegaCorp I left, and I struggled (as have others who have left the MegaCorp with similar specialty) to explain this unique skill and its benefits. The simplest (yes, this is simplest) way to describe it is Multi-disciplinary Product Strategist that integrates 1) end user/shopper/buyer understanding/insights, 2) business models, brand identity and business needs, and 3) product/package technologies and design. Clear as mud, hmm?

So, even with creating my own LLC, and signing on rosters with three different consulting groups (including YourEnore, which understands my specialty area), I wasn't seeing that path creating a flow of mentally stimulating project work.

I decided to take the path I had not taken - an Encore Career. Being able to say I am a Life Coach certainly helps with an identity statement. After taking two online courses, I am now a Certified Life Coach with a Certification for Retirement Life Coaching as well. To be honest, I am not sure how far down this path I will go. Is it my passion, my purpose? Not sure. But it certainly feels good to be able to answer the question, "What do you do?"

Because my needs are more emotional than financial, I am also looking into New Adventures to see if some of the emotional needs can be met through these types of pursuits

BLOG POST: Herd Mentality Blog Post

It's hard to acknowledge that I follow a herd mentality. Life is defined by social norms. As social animals, we find life easier and more comfortable to adhere to group roles or mimic group behavior – it promotes safety, saves energy, and the approval is a source of pleasure.

Given that almost my entire social sphere is still working, I'm more comfortable with being perceived as a part-time, freelance worker. I "fit in" if I'm working. It allows me to keep a part of my former identity and the validation that comes with that identity. And being an early retiree, my work colleagues all assumed I would continue to work. So, since retiring, I've continued to work part-time as a consultant in my field of expertise.

Last May, I got caught up in the work, not thinking about life. I returned to the regular habits of years – juggling multiple projects, loving the fact I was being asked my opinion on things, but also not exercising, not blogging, not connecting with friends. Yes, I returned to my workaholic habits.

And I didn't like it at all.

It's hard to be different from your social sphere. I'm not sure how to give up part-time work. Since I struggle with the workaholic tendencies, I think I need to. I've realized I don't know how to "fit in" with friends or even how to live life if I'm not working as part of it. Should I give up the part-time work or not?

How do I find a new herd mentality to become part of? How do I find a social sphere of (young-ish) retirees who are not working? Will this give me alternative role models to help me feel like part-time work is not the must do to fit in?

Learning Moment – **Are boomers really all working?**

Time for a reality check: all retirees do not work! While about 50% of Baby Boomers have stated they plan to work in retirement, the numbers don't (yet) play out. Retirement Options, (a retirement coaching firm created by Richard P. Johnson Ph.D.) claims that only 47% of men and 34% of women aged sixty-two to sixty-four are working (including part-time). That drops to 30% of men and 20% of women by ages sixty-five to sixty-nine. So working in retirement is a choice, not an expectation.

MY DOMAIN SUMMARY:
WORK/CAREER INSIGHTS and IDEAS:

_____

_____

_____

_____

_____

_____

_____

_____

CHAPTER 7

MY RETIREMENT LIFESTYLE
LOCATION & LEISURE DOMAINS

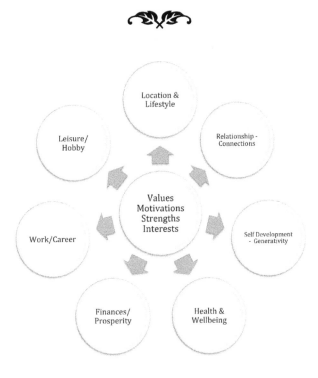

LOCATION, LOCATION. . . .LIFESTYLE

Where to live is the #2 question most retirees have! But to answer that, you need to think about what kind of lifestyle you want to live. While the mantra for purchasing a home seems to be "location,

location, location," I have found that in Retirement Transition, the decision on where to live is more "location, location. . . . <u>lifestyle</u>!"

There are as many assumptions about retirement "where to live" as there are people. Some assume they will move to Florida, North Carolina, Arizona or some other "retirement mecca." I received the *Where to Retire* magazine that was built on this premise for a few years!

Some retirees assume they will move to where their kids live (and follow their kids' career moves?). Some assume they will stay in their current location, but downsize, maybe into a condo or retirement community. I know a few who resized bigger in their current location to accommodate grandkids' visits! Some assume they will simply stay in place. Aging in place is a newly established phrase that requires its own set of considerations.

And finally, if you are part of a couple, there is the consideration of both of you in answering some of the critical questions, especially if considering relocation:

Connection to Family and Friends

There is a big difference between someone who has lived in one place for twenty-five-plus years and someone who has moved every five to seven years. Do you enjoy getting to know new people? Do you have the skillset to move and easily make new friends? (I find "military kids" have that skill well developed!). I have spoken to a few retirees who moved to another state and then struggled with establishing a new set of friends.

What about family? Do we want to be close to relatives/aging parents? What is your personal connection with friends and family, and how do you see it in the future? How important is it to be near family and friends? Do you want friends and family to regularly visit?

Lifestyle Considerations

What lifestyle do you want to live? Does the location provide access to activities of interest and/or job opportunities for that lifestyle? Do you like participating in groups, clubs, and organizations? Explore new places/try new things? Do you love to go to the theater/concerts, nightlife, restaurants, sporting events, and/or cultural activities? Will you be working in the future? Volunteering? Does the location have the right opportunities for the lifestyle you want to live?

Environmental Dynamics

Are you more about being close to the urban core activities and energy or close to nature and the outdoors? Is walkability important? Safety? Diversity? What kind of "vibe" do you want – friendly neighbors, mixed ethnicity, specific ideologies?

What climate do you love or hate? Dry versus humid? Do you love seasonal changes, the water, the mountains, or the desert?

Accessibility

Especially if relocating, or even considering where you currently live, what is the access to health care? A retired friend moved from the country to the city core – being over an hour from the nearest hospital, as her husband's health declined, became a constant worry.

Do you need to address possible physical limitations of aging (i.e., stairs, bathroom design)?

What about access to transportation - airport for travel or local infrastructure/mass transit as we age? How important is access to IRL educational opportunities?

Financial Considerations

Is there a budget restriction? Are there financial considerations on cost of living, taxes, capital tied up in real estate, taxes? Have you considered ongoing maintenance – whether it's being physically able to do it or paying for it?

Crazy Options

Have you considered alternative living possibilities: RV living, international living, multi-generational living, dual location?

If you are looking into splitting locations (snow birds), does one become an income producer and how does that fit into your lifestyle vision? One retiree I spoke with has a beach condo but needs to rent it in-season to help pay for it, so she is never there in the "good months." Another couple worries because they have heard stories about renting and the place getting "trashed."

HOW-TO COOL TOOL: "What is Home?"

This tool is expanded based on a concept found in *What Color is Your Parachute in Retirement* by John E. Nelson and Richard N. Bolles. In retirement, you (both if part of a couple) will probably be spending more time at home. Clarifying what "home" means to you (and others in the same space), or what you want it to mean, can be helpful.

Which of the following statements best fits?

- My home reflects me. I am the caretaker, handy-person, house-keeper, and/or groundskeeper and that is personally rewarding. Home improvement and renovation are personally rewarding.
- My home is my studio for my hobby/crafts/passion projects. I need the work space to reflect my creative needs.
- My home is the storage (warehouse) and/or display (showcase) for my physical possessions.
- My home is a community center and open 24/7. It is my personal entertainment and social connection hub for gathering of all sorts, or a bunkhouse/camp for family visits.
- My home is my personal retreat. It contains my personal refuge for privacy and serenity.
- My home is simply the base of operation - my base camp from which to explore the world.

REAL LIFE EXAMPES: We have retiree friends who view their retirement home as a base camp - just someplace to rest their heads between their travels and activities. They adore their one-bedroom condo where they can "lock the door and leave" on various trips. Another retiree friend built a five-bedroom home with a play area and pool so her grandkids could visit regularly. And another retired couple determined that condo living was not right because the grill-master needed space to cook outside; they adore their new home with its large patio.

Our personal couple's conversation also answered the question: <u>Is this a ten-year plan or the final move plan?</u> This was a big mindset shift for us as early-retirees. Our next 'where to live' did not need to consider age-in-place requirements but rather was more about current lifestyle considerations! Our "What is Home?" conversation indicated that I want a home that is a community/entertainment center, while he wants a storage facility. So our search for our next ten-year home became more a "resize" from our current one with its small kitchen and garage.

BLOG POST: Sense of Place

Relocation is a big part of many retirement transitions, and it was part of my retirement vision. While our new home is downsized (from 4 bed, 4.5 bath to a 2 bed, 2.5 bath), it is still three stories and actually has more steps leading into it (eight steps up to the front porch). It is definitely not an age-in-place type of accommodation, nor does it lend itself to becoming one. It is not in Florida; it is not closer to or farther from family; it is about six miles from our previous home. It is not a condo; we still have yard work to do. So many have asked: Why did I need to move?

I needed to move for very personal reasons. Our old house had me mentally shackled. It was purchased at a very different (and difficult) time of our life for very different lifestyle requirements. While I learned to appreciate living there with its big rooms, random-width wood floors, and coved ceilings, the kitchen never felt comfortable for me to cook in, so I've gotten out of the habit of cooking. Even with ten rooms, there was no space in it that I felt was really mine. The house, in fact, never felt like it was mine. It didn't give me a sense of place.

I'm not usually a touchy-feely kind of person; I'm an engineer by training and analytical by nature. But the new house has a welcoming feel - a feeling that it's mine (and hubby's).

I'm not usually a touchy-feely kind of person; I'm an engineer by training and analytical by nature. But the new house has a welcoming feel - a feeling that it's mine (and hubby's).

I've also been asked if I have a sense of loss moving away from the old house we've lived in for sixteen years, the longest house in our married life and almost the longest I've ever lived in. While I will miss the neighbors, I don't miss the house itself. While it does have a few design features I miss (master bathroom, screened-in porch, country sink), I will not miss the busy street, the almost impossible to manage hilly sideyard or the old plumbing.

I am looking forward to beginning a new stage of life in our new space, where I do feel a sense of place. And the stained glass windows, bigger kitchen, and front porch on a quiet street all help.

Do you have a sense of place where you live?

LEISURE/ HOBBY DOMAIN
Learning How to Play

I knew I wanted my next stage of life to be "more play and less work," which means creating a strong understanding of how my Leisure/ Hobby Life Domain would come to life. When I created my first life vision with this framework, initially the Leisure/Hobby domain was almost empty! My pre-retirement life was 90% work-focused.

It's a bit frightening to realize that at age fifty-plus, I had no idea how to play! Part of me needed to overcome the strong Protestant work ethic I was raised on - working hard is practically part of my DNA! Taking time to play was just not something I'd really ever done. So I needed to learn how to play.

What exactly is leisure? What hobbies could I begin to develop? In true researcher fashion, I have done a deep review of leisure, hobby, and play. Leisure (play) is a wide area and is not independent of activities that would fit in other Life Domains, like Health & Wellbeing. I have also found that leisure is about "doing" - whether that is passive doing (reading, eating, watching) or active doing (walking, swimming).

A LEISURE FRAMEWORK - Here are some of the categories that can be considered Leisure/Play with some examples (not an all-encompassing list and yes, one activity can hit a few categories):

Creative Expression - Personal Artistry	Writing, painting, making music, dancing, jewelry making, crafting, cooking, flower arranging, quilting, woodworking, home décor, etc.
Physical Activity - Exercise and Beyond	Walking, biking, hiking, standup paddle boarding, tennis, Zumba, golf, dance lessons, running, cardio work out, strength training, gardening, play sports, learn to swim, learn to sail, etc.
Intellectual Stimulation - Learning New Things/Skills	Visit museums, attend lectures, take local university classes, online classes, podcasts in topics that interest you: chess, birding, cooking, architecture, new language, mysticism, astronomy, etc.
Social Interaction	Book club, dining out, happy hour, explore meetup.com, visit with friends/neighbors, play cards, club meetings, etc.
Solitary Relaxation	Yoga, journaling, reading, crosswords, coloring books, listen to music, scrapbooking, meditation, etc.
Spectator Appreciation	Movies, concerts, art gallery walks, theater, following sports, craft shows, bird watch, etc.
Travel Experiences	Stay-cation activities, big trip travel planning, vocation vacation, active vacations, cruises/tours, Road Scholar, etc.

REAL LIFE EXAMPLE: I found looking at a broad range of leisure activities/pursuits in this fashion quite helpful! While this approach might feel a bit absurd, I really did need to learn what leisure was. Choosing ones that fit my vision of living an active, healthy lifestyle, as well as my passive interest areas of observing art and playing with words (personal interest spaces) took time. In some of these leisure activities I am very much a beginner; in some, I am experimenting with the activity – "trying it on." I am finding a lot of enjoyment in learning to play!

MY DOMAIN SUMMARIES:
<u>LOCATION & LIFESTYLE INSIGHTS and IDEAS</u>

_____
_____
_____
_____
_____
_____
_____
_____
_____
_____

<u>LEISURE FRAMEWORK INSIGHTS and IDEAS</u>

_____
_____
_____
_____
_____
_____
_____
_____
_____

CHAPTER 8

A HEALTHY LIFESTYLE
HEALTH & WELLBEING DOMAIN

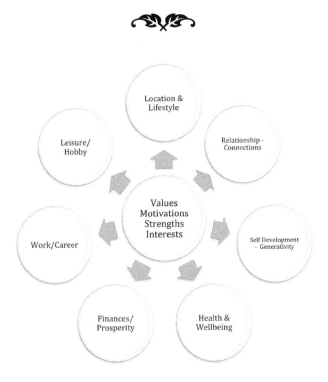

LIVING A HEALTHY LIFESTYLE

Health & Wellbeing is another Life Domain that I needed to explore more deeply as I worked through my retirement transition. It was interesting how many retirement books and blogs mentioned this area as important, although I didn't find any that addressed it in depth.

I found lots of references to the commonly held healthy living guidelines - seven to eight hours of sleep, eight glasses of water every day, 10,000 steps a day, five fruits veggies a day, regular check-ups with your doctor(s), the appropriate screening diagnostics/shots for your age, management of your innate health condition(s), etc. But I also found some references to other aspects of health and wellbeing like the spiritual side, connections to others, and mental (brain) stimulation, especially as you age and leave behind the highly mind-stimulating work environment.

A synthesized framework to explore Health & Wellbeing Domain in this next life stage is offered below. It is holistic to capture the mind, body, and soul. It addresses not only the physical changes that are coming with aging, but the loss of social and mental aspects that can come when leaving a traditional work environment. And yes, many aspects of Health & Wellbeing are not independent of other Life Domains like Relationships, Leisure/Hobbies and Work/Career.

A HEALTH & WELLBEING FRAMEWORK

	Domain Sub-Areas	Possible Action Spaces
MIND – Mental Wellbeing	Mental stimulation and lifelong learning; Stress management; Social connection, interactions and intimacy	Brain Stimulation Play Often Have Fun Connect with Others
BODY – Physical Wellbeing	Movement and physical fitness; Nutrition and hydration; Relaxation and sleep	Move It Eat Well Hydrate Enough Sleep Soundly
SOUL – Spiritual Wellbeing	Personal Purpose; Positivity; Community connection and volunteerism; Spirituality and religious beliefs	Be Mindful Laugh Often

Here's a bit more on a few possible ideas in considering aspects of your own Health & Wellbeing domain:

- <u>Move it</u> – It's about activity and physical movement, but also about strength and flexibility. Essentially, less time sitting! Even if you like to read and write, balance this with being out in nature, doing yard work, or taking a walk. And yes, it's both aerobic/cardio as well as strength training. Exploring matching "Move it" activities to your personality. A mostly introverted personality can explore solo sports like walking, biking, swimming, and (maybe) rock climbing. Or group exercises that still allow a quiet, centered place like yoga, Pilates or even weight circuits while watching TV. Extroverts, however, can find some interest in group sports (tennis, pickle-ball), fitness classes (Zumba, NIA), and meetup.com groups (hiking, paddle-boarding, and dancing).

- <u>Eat Well</u> – The benefits of healthy eating habits are huge – managing weight, boosting energy, reducing risk of disease. And, there are so many guidelines. But, unfortunately, knowing the "rules" doesn't make following them any easier! Here's some to consider trying:
  - o <u>Don't skip breakfast</u>. And "coffee only" is skipping breakfast. This was a habit I got into while working since so often morning work meetings had food associated with them, and I have no willpower when faced with fresh bagels. And I'm not a morning person to get up and make a real breakfast. But still, try to have a morning meal every day.
  - o <u>Be more plant-based</u> with lots of fruits and veggies and whole grains. I have a friend who swears by her five colorful servings of veggies a day. Yes, having carrot sticks in the fridge, apples on the counter and freshly roasted pumpkin seeds available do help when the munchies occur!
  - o <u>Minimize the bad stuff</u> – fats, sugars, fried foods, processed food, and carbs. Notice I said minimize versus eliminate! I love bread, fries, pasta and a great charcuterie board. Those are food groups unto themselves, right? But I am trying to eat them more in moderation – and only really good bread, really good fries, and really good pasta. Because if you're

gonna have a bad food group, have a really good bad food group! Preferably with wine, also in moderation.

o <u>Watch portion size. Stay hydrated</u>. I put these two together because to me they are both about limiting intake. I've learned that sometimes, it's not that I'm hungry, but that I'm thirsty! When I stay hydrated and eat good food, it is easier to watch portion size. When the food is good, I want to savor it, which slows my eating and my tummy has time to tell my brain "you are full."

- <u>Use it</u> – Brain stimulating activities are so important when you no longer have the "daily problems to solve" activity of the workplace. As you also don't have the daily stresses and hassles of the workplace, this is not a bad trade-off. It's been a joy to find mind-stimulating things that are fun, too! Reading, writing, and crosswords have all found their way into my regular routines. I've seen reference to playing music as a great mind stimulator as well, (but for me long ago piano lessons and guitar lessons were more frustrating than joyful.) I am thinking about trying chess or jewelry making. What brain stimulating things fit your interests?

- <u>Find Fun</u> – The quote "fly while you still have wings – go places, do things" really hit home for me as I spoke with some retirees that, similar to my own dad, had debilitating health issues arise quite soon after retirement, causing them to re-think their retirement years quite significantly. I know I am blessed with wings right now, and I need to run and play, laugh and have fun. I'm creating the lists of places to go (both locally and globally), things to experience (events, foods, theater), hobbies to try, and areas to explore (learning), and then doing a quarterly plan.

- <u>Connect with Others</u> – I knew, rationally, that many of my work-based connections would slowly disappear in retirement. Most social connections are based on convenience, whether it is school or work or where you live. And since work dominated my life, my work-based connections dominated. But the reality of the void leaving work created was bigger than anticipated. I am consciously adding in relationship generator activities to establish a new "convenience" space, which I hope will lead to new connections, from support networks to friendships.

- <u>Be Mindful</u> – As a Type-A action-focused workaholic, it has been a learning experience to be more mindful, slow down and allow the days to unfold. To me mindfulness has been to consciously take time for personal reflection with reading and journaling, becoming a learner taking classes, finding joy in a hobby where I have no mastery, and spending time in nature.

A friend who knows I was looking deeply into retirement transition asked me about Aging and <u>Health Care</u>. And, once again, I could not point her to an in-depth review on this! I guess it comes down to <u>know the signs/symptoms of, and get the screenings for, the common aging issues</u> (heart health, osteoporosis, breast cancer, Alzheimer's, arthritis, skin cancer, other cancers, depression, etc.). I have put "personal health check-ups" on my life maintenance plan, along with the house AC service, quarterly financial review, and car oil changes. Keep everything running smoothly.

Health & Wellbeing is an important domain in my Life Plan, so I am intentional in all three of its aspects (mind, body, and soul) in my action plan. What is your intentional action plan in this domain?

MY DOMAIN SUMMARY:
<u>HEALTH & WELLBEING INSIGHTS and IDEAS</u>

_____

_____

_____

_____

_____

_____

_____

_____

_____

CHAPTER 9

WHO AM I?

RELATIONSHIP &
SELF-DEVELOPMENT DOMAINS
(AND AN ASIDE ON FINANCES)

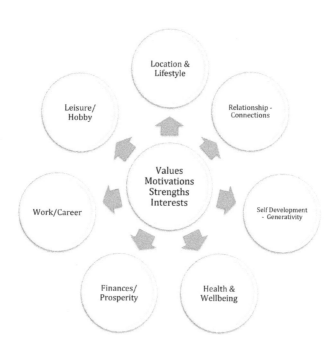

(RE)ESTABLISHING A RELATIONSHIP PROFILE

Al l the books and blogs on retirement agree: active, healthy relationships are critical for healthy aging.

There are four major relationship areas in a person's life, and the transition to retirement can stress, change, or eliminate your relationship profile overnight. As with all my transitioning, understanding how my relationship profile was changing and addressing the changes required personal reflection, exploring options, and moving to action.

Through any major life transition, friendships decline as the circumstances of your life change. Most relationships happen because of our surroundings – where we live, work and play. As you leave the work environment with its easy proximity to relationship building, move location, or change your daily habits, it's important to create more natural opportunities to be social with others.

Social Friends – There is a phrase about friends: "Friends for a season, friends for a reason, and friends for life."

Most social connections are based on convenience, school or work, or where you live. Most of these could be considered your "season" friends with the life convenience element part of that life season. There are the soccer moms, your kid's friends' parents, the work-based connections, or neighbors where you live or hang out. More than acquaintances but linked more by life's seasons. When the convenience of the proximity is gone, so too goes the friendship.

Friends for a reason are the friends who are linked to common interests. "Season" friends can become "reason" friends through reciprocity and interdependence where you both contribute and receive in the relationship. You are better when together, comfortable to be yourself, and it's soul enhancing. They know you; you know them. You talk, whether it's over wine, over steps, or over the Internet (posts and comments). These are the friends who, when things get tough in life, they are there. They are the ones who keep you accountable, the ones who support you, the ones who you have fun with, season after season.

What about friends for life? I heard once that this group is maybe two to five people – the "you can count them on one hand" friends. It is the person you call at 2 AM because you need someone. This is the friend who lasts through the seasons (life stages), and through the reasons (changing hobbies, changing interests, changing locations). I have two to four people on this list. Two for sure I would call no matter what, and two I do feel I could call, but probably wouldn't. I'm not sure how folks get into this category except through time. . . this one requires time.

Professional Relationships – Work colleagues are often just professional relationships that we mistake for social friends. However, work connections provide many of our daily conversations - idea builders, cheerleaders, devil's advocates, and validation of actions taken. Work provided the casual conversations about what is happening in your life, from an update on the kitchen re-do to vacation plans to a family/personal challenge, and provided moments that validated and made you feel like you are not alone.

And when the work convenience is gone, many of those relationships just don't have common ground anymore. Yes, work ends, everyone says they will stay in touch, but it really doesn't happen with most co-workers. You don't want to be the living ghost coming back to haunt the halls. Replacing not only these mind-stimulating debates but the daily what's-up conversations is a huge component of retirement transition. What to do with all those (now silent) hours of the day?

Family – I know many women who enter retirement only to become a primary caregiver - to grandkids or aging parents/parents-in-law. Even with no kids and only one parent still living, how would having more time available change family relationships?

Spouse – One of the most significant relationships to work on through transition is your spouse, partner, or significant other relationship. Are you both retiring? How would more time at home change dynamics and house routines? When time apart is no longer structured as you go to your separate work environments, how do you think about time together and time apart?

REAL LIFE EXAMPLE: I recognized quickly that I needed an intentional relationship action plan to recreate the support network that I naturally had at work – my work "season" was over. Work was my tribe, my herd, my village! Without it, I did not have many active, healthy relationships. I needed to create moments of connection, to establish (re-establish) and build (new) relationships. Who was I going to talk to every day? Who was going to be my cheerleader, my positive critic? Who could be my accountability buddy, my "partner in crime," my reality checker? How would I use my new free time to reconnect with old friends and strengthen the friendships I did have? This intentional plan had weekly/monthly goals - number of people to contact, activities to plan. Sounds like work? Maybe. Even three years into retirement, this continued to be a personal challenge. But I come back to the statement I started with - active, healthy relationships are critical for healthy aging.

Here are some elements you might be able to re-apply:

- **Creating a coupledom vision.** I am quite fortunate that my marriage was one of the healthy relationships I did have. Hubby remains my best friend and in retirement we do enjoy spending more time together. But he's often living the issues and stories and certainly doesn't want to hear about them! We needed to come to a shared vision on many of the Life Domains, like where would we live, relationships besides our own (friends and family connections), pleasure plans (travel, toys), and work or not. But one of the most challenging aspects, and one we are continually working on, is the time together/time apart balance. Regular conversation helps. Some of those conversations were about exploring some new things together and re-evaluating household task distribution. But we try to be the biggest supporter/encourager in the new activities for the other, choose to continue life commitment to each other, remember why we fell in love in the first place. It's not 50/50; it's a 200/100 – give it all you've got.

- **Active networking.** Let me remind you, I am an introvert, so the concept of active networking is really difficult. But it is necessary for achieving my future life vision. I plan two to four Quarterly Networking Meetings - everything from coffee chats, lunch catch-ups or happy hour to going to full-on networking meetings with lots of people. I had a few work-based relationships that I hoped would survive the transition and thrive into social friends. Networking takes scheduling and sometimes thinking through what to talk about, especially as I reach out to colleagues I didn't know that well but are doing things now that I find intriguing. But it has also been a case of planned serendipity. I've gotten ideas for blogs, classes, and travel. And it does keep my mind stimulated as we often talk about the corporate world or I get to do some mentoring and advising on things they are working on.

- **Fun with Friends - old and new.** This started out as Food & Friends since being a "foodie" is in my life vision. I love a good meal with friends - new foods to explore and great conversation are my ideal connection. But this turned into too many eating out moments. So I had to work to have shared communal activities that are beyond meals and increase the regularity of being in different surroundings to create circumstances to meet and interact with like-minded individuals. Walks in the park, going to events, taking a class. I am not giving up on Food & Friends, just thinking about finding more shared activities that both rekindle "old" friendships and allow the formation of new relationships that can be nurtured into friendships. Again, this requires active scheduling and watching for opportunities. I now have a regular set of Women-Who-Walk friends. From monthly to weekly, weather dependent, we walk and chat, combining connection and physical activity – a two for one. And hubby and I still keep up with our Foodie Friends, exploring new restaurants around town on a regular basis.

- **Embrace technology.** For years I was a "Facebook stalker," merely reading what's up with family and friends. Now I try to comment and post, interact and feel more connected. I entered the world of blogging similarly – not just reading, but actively commenting. My blogging community is a new set of virtual friends who provide inspiration and encouragement. Both of these social media connections are creating an outer-circle of connections for me – people around the world with whom I converse and share ideas. And in the continuous learning mode, I did try Instagram and Twitter, but I am still a total beginner (i.e., clueless) on both of these formats!

Summarizing Connections.

Some learning on investing the time for friendship development:
- Take responsibility to find new friends. Take action. Choose those surroundings to match your areas of interest and be consistent in the activity.
- Not all attempts to create more relationships will be successful. Joining a philanthropic group left me with a third-wheel feeling as everyone else joined up as existing friends. One local yoga studio is more a come, do it and leave; it was four months of regular attendance before one instructor even asked for my name. But keep trying new things as something will click.
- Recognize that new friendships, new support systems, and a new sense of community take time to develop. Invest the time, be patient.
- All new relationships won't gel into friendships. A real friend is when the two of you become better in each other's presence. There is affinity, affection, and concern; you're completely at ease with that person.
- One area I have struggled with in friendship development is reciprocity. I feel like I am always the initiator with so many acquaintances I am trying to nurture into friendships. But

perseverance is one of my strengths, so I will continue on this path, trying to understand each relationship and cultivate it. When I began thinking about the investment (my time, thinking, and planning) as a gift to them, and I do enjoy the time we are together, it became a win-win.

SELF-DEVELOPMENT and GENERATIVITY DOMAIN

This domain is a mish-mash of a few different topics often cited about adult development. Many people at this retirement transition stage of their life feel a need to "give back" and/or to "grow more" as an individual. Some might relate this to purpose or legacy. There are two different frameworks that capture these needs: Erik Erikson's eight-stage psychosocial theory of development and Robert Kegan's five stages of adult development.

Erikson Theory and Volunteering

Erik Erikson (1902-1994) proposed an eight-stage psychosocial theory of development. During each developmental stage, two conflicting ideas must be resolved in order for an individual to become a confident, contributing member of society. Failure to master the developmental stage results in feelings of inadequacy.

"Generativity versus Stagnation" is the seventh of eight stages of Erik Erikson's theory of psychosocial development and takes place during middle adulthood, which correlates strongly with retirement/early retirement. Generativity refers to making your mark on the world by creating or nurturing things that will outlast you. This might have come through your primary career of productive work or raising your children, but might not. Or you might feel a need to continue or do more. Becoming involved in community activities or volunteer organizations can be a way to master this developmental stage.

Volunteering can come in different forms in retirement. There can be unpaid caregiving for family members, grandkids, or friends; continued mentoring of colleagues; or active engagement in community or church activities. There can also be more formal volunteering.

If looking at formal volunteer work, it's important to find an opportunity that's right for you. Find an opportunity that matches your desires, skills, interests, and schedule.

- First, understand your <u>personal motivation for volunteering</u>. Is it the desire to give back to the community and make a difference; or is it to improve one's own life and health; or to meet new peers and expand one's social network/feel like part of a community; or to try something new, learn new skills or experience a sense of adventure? The volunteer possibilities are endless, so understanding your own motivation is critical, including <u>the time commitment you want to make</u>. Do you want to make a commitment to tutor a young student, for example, building a close relationship that may extend over several years? Or are you more interested in single-shot opportunities that might engage you for a few weeks or months?

- Second, brainstorm a list of <u>causes and/or areas you are passionate about</u> - things like animals, children, the elderly, political change, the environment, or disease awareness. Then think about what <u>skills or talent you might have</u> to lend to an organization. What are you good at and what do you like to do? Your list can include tasks like office work, helping people, or manual labor. Getting clear on your desires, interests, and skills will help you in the next step – searching for an organization.

Once you have an idea of why and what, you can look into churches, schools, health organizations/hospitals, community service, civic and political organizations, sports and environmental groups to find an opportunity. Use your existing network of friends and community contacts. Take advantage of the many nonprofit clearinghouses like the United Way, Impact 100, an online volunteer connector, or other larger organization that has exposure to many different organizations.

Kegan's Adult Development

Slightly different than Erikson, Robert Kegan's work presents an increasing complexity of consciousness development in Five Stages of Adult Development (briefly summarized below). He identifies that some adults never go beyond Stage 2, most are in Stage 3, and very few reach Stage 5. I found Stage 4 the most intriguing:

Stage 1 – the Impulsive Mind	It's all about the now; what is present; I want it & I want it now. Child-like behavior.
Stage 2 – the Imperial Mind	It's all about me & my needs, interests, agenda; competitive, rules-based, self-interest groups; care what others think b/c impacts getting my needs met; follow rules b/c fear punishment or want reward (not b/c believe in values that the rules represented); need respect. Solidly the "teen years."
Stage 3 – the Socialized Mind	It's how it's done; rules, regulations & norms; external societal beliefs & social expectations shape sense of self; you care about others' opinions b/c others are source of validation – authority, acceptance, orientation/identity, guidance; with others it's about mutual rewards/ mutual satisfaction; feel personally responsible for others' experience; relationships are reason I exist (I am me because you are you); team player; promises made/ promises kept; believe in right & wrong (values)
Stage 4 – the Self-Authoring Mind	I define who I am (not others' definition, not societal norms); internal independent ownership of thinking/ own set of values defines actions; critical questioning to understand the complexity of different ideologies; self-reflective/self-discovery (this is what I stand for, this is my path); non-judgmental; confident in own abilities; relationships are part of world
Self-Transforming Mind	Interconnectedness and interdependence of everything; open to possibilities; constantly changing self

Stage 4 felt like a shift in personal development for this retirement transition stage! How can I learn to do what matters to me and not care what I think others think/expect? How can I stop feeling guilty for not doing the "should" or what's expected? How can I give up comparisons against others that lead to feelings of inferiority? Kegan shares ideas on how to achieve Stage 4:

- Spend time in self-discovery and self-reflection, defining and reshaping what you believe (your values, your beliefs), your sense of self and relationship to others.
  - o Be able to articulate – this is Who I am.

- o You are what you believe you are, so create the affirmations to change your (self-limiting) beliefs if necessary.
- o Clearly determine what you think so you can shift away from worry about what others think.
- Make sure your personal actions (what plan to do/what actually do) align with values. Shift from doing things you think others expect, to <u>doing things that align with the person you want to be, the values important to you.</u>
  - o Clarify what you believe are the actions associated with values. For example: If I value friendship, how do I know someone is a good friend? What defines friendship to me? And then, am I doing things that align with that?
  - o You do not need to do things to prove you love someone or anything you feel obligated to do or to meet others' expectations. You need to do things that match what is important to you, your values.
  - o How much dissonance is there between what you say you want (vision aligned with values) and how you actually behave (activities, time and energy spent)? This is looking for alignment or difference between intention (plans) and action (real behavior).

Essentially, clarify what is really important to you, commit yourself to pursue the activities that bring that to life, and stop doing things that are not linked to what's important. Recognize <u>we are all unique</u>, and what is right for you might not be right for me (and vice versa). So turn feelings of envy into admiration and inspiration. But inspiration only if what I'm admiring fits within my values, strengths, and motivations.

The traditional retirement is considered to be a thing of the past. The older retiree stereotype of working for one company, living frugally/saving well, and retiring to a lifestyle of leisure activities and a snowbird lifestyle is no longer a singular valid profile. The 21st Century Lifestyle Retirement is considered to be more about creative pursuits, second careers, urban lifestyles, personal growth, and giving back. Whether it's about Erikson's Generativity or Kegan's Self-Authoring Mind, I encourage you to better understand how you feel about this life domain. I personally struggle with legacy and generativity. I am coming to believe more the Kegan model and that my purpose is the full expression of who I am. . . lived out in my hobbies, relationships, and activities.

AN ASIDE on the FINANCES DOMAIN

A word or two on finances (even though this book does not address Financial Planning for Retirement!): <u>money in retirement is a foundation for the life you want to lead, a tool to accomplish your life goals.</u>

Some goals will require spending, but many will not. How many goals you select that require spending will depend on your personal cash flow assessments. Spending money in retirement can remind you of why you engaged in a wealth building first phase of life. Or you might be more limited in your cash flow. <u>Don't ignore this domain; it is needed as part of the full assessment phase.</u>

Since I didn't plan on a significant change in standard of living, and our cash flow assessments looked fine, this was not a critical assessment element for me. But as I've read the financial portions of the retirement books, I recognize my husband and I are not typical retiring Baby Boomers – we were the "rational agents" of the financial model, both saving money and not borrowing too heavily. The more common Baby Boomer characteristic was collectively to spend yesterday's money (savings) and spend tomorrow's money (borrow) as well as spend today's money (paycheck). We, however, saved extensively for retirement, living well within our means during our working years and being careful with investments. We also both worked for good, solid companies for many years. And, we are not supporting aging parents or boomerang kids. Yes, untypical!

I did make sure we were both very aware of where our financial resources were, what we expected to spend monthly/annually going forward (budgeting plans), and how the cash flow would be going forward (drawdown strategies). And we plan to review this every six months.

<u>Next, don't ignore your finances</u> - Work with a financial planner if needed to best understand your financial situation and make sure both you and your spouse/partner are aware of all the details (if applicable). Just remember there is more than "the money."

MY DOMAIN SUMMARIES:
<u>RELATIONSHIP INSIGHTS and IDEAS</u>

_____
_____
_____
_____
_____

<u>SELF-DEVELOPMENT and GENERATIVITY INSIGHTS</u>

_____
_____
_____
_____

<u>FINANCE INSIGHTS and ACTIONS</u>

_____
_____
_____
_____
_____

CHAPTER 10

CRAFTING THE VISION
REFLECT OUTPUT

There are many terms for a life vision – your mission, your purpose, your calling, your passion, your life meaning. Or even simply your vision of what's important to you, what brings you satisfaction. Some of these terms feel very weighty.

But getting to the vision statement of what you want your retirement lifestyle to be is what is needed. . . .the statement of <u>who to be and what I want the future to look like and then writing it down</u>, or actively visualizing it in some way. If I don't know who I want to become, how will I get there?

> *"Would you tell me please which way*
> *I should go from here?" said Alice.*
> *"That depends a good deal on*
> *where you want to get to," said the Cat.*
> Lewis Carroll in **Alice in Wonderland**

To create a retirement life that is fulfilling (the life I want to live) and become who I want to be, required me to define it, articulate it, visualize it! This was NOT easy. . . unlocking this inspirational destination can take storytelling, envisioning, some rethinking of personal branding, and some life coaching moments! But I do believe, when the destination/vision is clear in your mind/written down, serendipity will "take over"!

First – PULL TOGETHER ALL YOUR SUMMARIES – looking for themes.

Domain	Key Ideas and Insights
Location & Lifestyle	
Relationship/Connections	
Self- Development/ Generativity	
Health & Wellbeing	
Work/Career	
Leisure/Hobby	
Finances/ Prosperity	

Second – Create your Vision

It can be a series of "I AM" statements. It can be a written purpose statement. It can be a story of the future or a vision board. Or all of the above. What it does is answer the questions: Who do I want to be? And what do I want my life to be like?

HOW-TO COOL TOOL – **Storytelling**

We all love to tell stories. We tell the story of what happened on the way to work, on the trip we took, how we got to where we are today. (Lots of hard work and a little luck?)

Imagine it is five years from now. . .tell/write the (short) story of how you got to where you are. What happened to make this (future reality) happen? Now, tell/write another story, and another one. Think about the life domains framework - What is your story for where your Career is five years from now? How did this Location & Lifestyle come to be? What happened in your life with Volunteering or Connections? Write four or five different possible future states.

HOW-TO COOL TOOL – **How to Create a Vision Board**

1. Pick up six to ten different kinds of magazines that you're "attracted to." I've gotten some of mine at the local half-price bookshop. I also use magazines I like reading – this year that's been *Real Simple, O Magazine*, and *Coastal Living*.

2. Then as you are thinking about "What do I want to happen this year, in five years, in ten years?" or "What is my vision for the future?" (pick the question that feels best for you), flip through and rip out pictures that you feel a connection with. Don't think too much – just keep the question in your head.

3. Using scissors and glue-stick, cut and paste your pictures onto a poster board, continuing to think about your question.

4. When you are done putting all the visuals in place, tell (write it down) the story of the vision board. Creating the narrative for the board after it's done provides your conscious interpretation of the pictures, metaphors, and colors.

5. I have also used dream interpretation (for example: ***Understand Your Dreams*** by Alice Anne Parker) on the visuals to help clarify what my subconscious is telling me about the answer to the question. Some folks like to name their board, and that becomes their word/phrase for the year.

REAL LIFE EXAMPLE:

I AM STATEMENTS:

I am an active person, leading a healthy lifestyle, experiencing new things, and savoring the moments of daily life.

I have an abundance of friendships.

I am allowing the latent adventurer and creative artist inside me to emerge.

I am physically active every day, practicing preventive behaviors, eating healthy, and managing my medical conditions.

I am living in a comfortable, welcoming house that fills our needs.

Possibility - Life as a Couple – You might not be entering this next life stage alone. It is recommended that each of you craft your own vision statements and then work through a joint vision. Are we aligned on big-picture elements of future vision? Do we need to re-loop to understand each other's Core Values? And then the details:

- o   Where will we live? How much will we travel?
- o   Are we aligned on finances. . . do we both understand where the money is and the money plans?
- o   Time together and apart? What are we doing together and how much time do we each need apart? Doing novel (new) things with your partner, things you are both interested in, can help improve intimacy and bonding.
- o   What about social life – are we aligned on how much time with family and friends? Extended family responsibilities?
- o   What about household tasks/roles?

REAL LIFE EXAMPLE: Our Couples Conversation touched on some pretty big topics:

Couple Identity and Time Together – We needed to recognize that a "natural balance" was not necessarily going to emerge, as our life visions were different. One of us is a huge structured planner while the other likes to more randomly putter with different things. One of us is more of a homebody, while the other wants to be out and about. We didn't really have many joint activities anymore, as work had taken over one of our lives. We had to look for some compromises and creative solutions!

We needed to discover new ways of spending time together. We had talked in the past of our "need to learn how to resort," our term for retirement leisure. We took tennis lessons together because we are not ready for golf, but have said maybe golf in the future. We are doing standup paddle boarding together, specialty foodie store shopping, and regular theater date nights. But even after three years, we continue to struggle a bit with the differences in our life visions; communication and compromise continue.

Relationship with Family – We both have a strong sense of responsibility and two challenging family situations. We talked often about how we were planning to manage them short-term and long-term. Finding a solution to one family situation was a stress-filled project and became a huge part of the first year's plan, derailing a number of our personal early life goals. Continued communication and acknowledgment of the stress was important for both of us.

COMPLETE REFLECT PHASE SUMMARY

REFLECT was about laying the foundational self-knowledge and making some priority calls as to what you will be taking with you through this transition into your next stage of life, what you will be letting go of, and what you want the future to look like.

At this point you should:

- Be able to articulate your high priority core VALUES.
- Know which SKILLS and STRENGTHS you want to take or develop in this next stage of life.
- Understand what MOTIVATES you.
- Have identified areas of INTEREST that could be fun to continue or explore.
- Have clarified the important ROLES you will have in the next stage of life.
- Have ideas and insights into your future LIFE DOMAINS.
- Have crafted a LIFE VISION statement and had joint "me, you, we" conversations if needed.

CHAPTER 11

IMAGINE THE POSSIBILITIES
IMAGINE PHASE

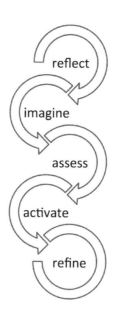

ALL THE POSSIBILITIES

More than just a task list of "honey-do" projects and going to those places you always wanted to visit (although those things are on it as well), IMAGINE is about creating a list of all the life possibilities you can think of, from passions to dreams to inklings; in work, leisure, volunteering; both active and passive activities; and any skills/talents you want to use or ones to learn or develop.

The concept of a possibilities list is similar to the Get-a-Life Tree exercise in the book by Ernie J. Zelinski called ***How to Retire Happy, Wild, and Free***. However, I've also heard it called a never-be-bored list by one retiree friend. Whatever you call it, this is about ideating possibilities, not assessing if they are the right ones to start doing.

When you're done you want to have created at least three pages worth of ideas - your goal is 100, if not 200 ideas! Your Personal Possibilities List will become your source of inspiration - to help bring clarity to what you want in your life (Life Plan), to create a daily/weekly/monthly plan, and/or to look to when you need a little push out of boredom.

Isn't this just my bucket list? Bucket lists tend to be "100 things to do/eat/see before I die" and could be pulled from your possibilities list! This list should be that and more – bits of who I want to "be," things I want to explore, etc. If having a traditional bucket list works for you, create it from, or incorporate into, this Possibilities List!

Imagining the possibilities.

There are many "life list" approaches (books/websites) that are quite helpful. I'm sharing exercises I felt worked best for me - a <u>range of brain-stimulating tasks and various sources of inspiration</u>. Pick ones that appeal to you.

As you go through these, don't make excuses to not put something on the list - no buts or I don't know how's. I do know that you will unconsciously filter things that just really have no interest for you. (I just do not want to jump out of a plane, ever.) If there is any even minor spark of interest, put it on your list!

After you have your list, you can do a few things with it. We will use it to choose activities that match your Life Vision statement (interests, strengths, values and life domains to focus on). You can use it to define some grand life goals. "Fifty states by the time I am fifty" was a grand goal earlier in my life. You can use it to look for patterns to create a "big plan" idea that might link multiple possibilities. But first, have fun creating the list!

COOL HOW TO TOOLS – Imagining Approaches

I encourage you to pick three or four of the below activities to craft your own Possibilities List.

- **Mind Mapping JOY** - What activities bring you joy today? What makes you lose track of time when you are engaged in it? What do you spend time doing when you can do anything? What activities brought you joy in the past? What old hobbies do you want to re-ignite?
- **Resolving Concerns** - What activities might help in your personal concern areas identified in Life Domains self-discovery?
  - o Activities that will get me physically fit. What activities would help get your body in shape? Change your eating habits? What are some physical pursuits you've always thought about trying? What sport have you wanted to learn to play?
  - o Activities that will create connection. How might I reconnect with friends you might not have had time for? Spend more time with family? Create new friendships?
  - o Activities that will stimulate my brain/personal development. What have I dreamed about trying/studying? What have people suggested you try?
- **Looking Back** - Looking at the past gives ideas for the future. Go back and look at old journals, previous life/bucket lists, or old to-do lists (if you have them). What did you like to do, want to do? Or ask family and/or old friends: What did I always want to do?
- **Scavenger Hunt** - Go to the bookstore and select five books/magazines on things you've never done (check the books for Dummies section). What are they? You might even buy them and explore! If nothing else, what sections in the bookstore did you drift to?
- **Looking Around** - Whose lifestyles do you/have you admired? What about them would you like to replicate in yours? I love A's food adventurism, K's devotion to exercise, M's search for wearable fashion, C's active stay-cation mindset summers.
- **Creative Spirit** - If you were to create a TV documentary or TV special or blog, what would it be about?

- **Imaginary Lives** - An exercise modified from ***The Artist's Way*** by Julia Cameron. If you could pick five to ten other lives to live, what would they be? Do not be sensible – list at least five that would be fun and exciting. Don't think about skills you need; focus on the excitement. To get you started, here's some I have seen on others' lists (including some that they actually tried): docent/tour guide, realtor, professor, painter, marathoner, kite flyer, park ranger, massage therapist, dancer, architecture buff, quilter, book writer, photographer, board member, start-up advisor, antique dealer, life coach, financial advisor, yoga teacher.
- **Places to Go, Things to Do, People to See** - What are the twenty-five destinations you have always wanted to visit (locally, domestically, internationally)? The twenty-five things you want to experience (foods to eat, people to meet, events to attend, books to read)? What is your "metro list" – the stay-cation/learn your city list – museums, boutiques, shows, festival, parks, restaurants, neighborhoods, outdoor art, etc?
- **If Only** - Fill in the blanks: Someday I would love to try X. If money were no object, I would try Y. If I knew I could be successful/competent at it, I would Z.

Some more approaches for ideas to add to your list:

HOW-TO COOL TOOL – Leisure Domains Lists
How would you like to <u>spend your leisure time</u>?

Creative Expression - Personal Artistry	Writing, painting, making music, dancing, crafting, cooking, flower arranging, wood-working, home décor(ing)
Physical Activity - Exercise and Beyond	Walking, biking, running, tennis, Zumba, golf, dance lessons, cardio work out, gardening, playing sports

Intellectual Stimulation - Learning New Things/Skills	Visit museums, attend lectures, play chess, bird watch, learn to cook, study architecture, acquire a new language, study astronomy, learn to sail
Social Interaction	Dining out, happy hour, visit with friends/neighbors, play cards, club meetings
Solitary Relaxation	Yoga, journaling, reading, crosswords, coloring books, listen to music, scrapbooking
Spectator Appreciation	Movies, concerts, art gallery walks, theater, following sports, craft shows, bird watch.
Travel Experiences	Stay-cation activities, big trip travel planning, adventure sports, vocation vacation, RoadScholar

HOW-TO COOL TOOL – Learning Topics

What would I like to <u>learn more about</u>?

History	Life sciences	Psychology
Current events	Spirituality	Languages
Physics	Design	Religion
Business	Entrepreneurship	Flying
Sports	Food and Nutrition	Massage
Dramatics	The Arts	Construction
Electronics	Computers	Coding
Finance	Architecture	Astronomy
Gardening	Genealogy	World Cultures
Writing	Boating	Geography
Philosophy	Literature	Music
The Brain	Photography	Wine

HOW-TO COOL TOOL – Activities List

What activities do you do today? What would <u>you like to try tomorrow?</u>

Acting/Dramatics	Gymnastics
Antiquing	Hiking/Walking
Attending auctions	Home decorating
Attending concerts	Home renovation/flipping
Attending flea markets/yard sales	Horseback riding
Auto racing	Horseshoes
Auto repairing	Hunting
Backpacking	Ice Skating
Baseball/Softball	Jewelry making
Basketball	Jigsaw puzzles
Bicycling	Jogging
Billiards/Pool	Judo/Karate
Bingo	Kite flying
Bird watching	Knitting/Crochet
Board Games	Listen to Podcasts
Boating	Listen to radio
Bookbinding	Mechanics
Bowling	Metalwork
Boxing	Model building
Bus tours	Motorcycling
Camping	Mountain climbing
Canoeing/Kayaking	Needlework
Card games	Painting/Drawing
Carpentry/woodworking	Parties
Casino gambling	Pets
Ceramics/Pottery	Photography
Chess	Playing musical instruments

Civic organizations
Collecting coins
Conservation/Ecology
Cooking/Baking
Crafts
Crossword puzzles
Dancing: Social
Darkroom work
Designing clothes
Dining out
Discussions
Drawing
Driving
Electronics
Embroidery
Encounter groups
Exercising
Fishing: Freshwater
Fishing: Saltwater
Flower arranging
Flying/Gliding
Folk dancing
Football
Gardening
Go to Ballet/Opera
Go to horse races
Go to movies
Go to nightclubs
Go to plays/lectures
Go to theater
Golf

Playing poker
Political activities
Reading
Religious organization
Rug Hooking
Sailing
Scrabble
Sewing
Shopping
Shuffleboard
Sightseeing
Singing
Skiing
Skin diving
Social drinking
Square dancing
Swimming
Table tennis
Talking on phone
Tennis
Traveling
Visit museums
Visiting friends
Volleyball
Volunteering
Watching team sports
Watching TV
Weaving
Weightlifting
Writing
Yoga

HOW-TO COOL TOOL – Possibilities Lists Based on Strengths

Strength	Possibility Ideas
Curiosity	Read a variety of blogs; explore different cultures (including the food); visit at least one new town/state/country a year; explore nature one hour/week; pick a new topic to study every year; create personal bucket lists for 100 foods to try, places to visit, things to see
Creativity	Write (articles, essays, blogs, short stories, poems); paint, sculpt; audition at local theater/choir; redesign room/house; take a class in pottery/glass blowing/photography/stained glass/knitting; design personalized cards; explore creative arts – Ikebana, Feng Shui, origami
Love of learning	Learn five new words a week; visit new museum or gallery every month; write about new things learned; read a non-fiction book monthly; follow global events (newspaper/Internet); join local book club; attend seminars in areas of interest; travel to new places
Bravery	Join an activist organization; write about a cause; volunteer with an organization devoted to a cause you believe in; participate in (peaceful) protests, work constructively for social change; join Peace Corps; go on missions to Third World countries
Healthy Vitality	Exercise three times a week; work on better "sleep hygiene"; engage in physically vigorous activities – bike riding, running, sports, singing, dancing; create/maintain relaxation/mediation routines
Love/ Nurture	Express love regularly (verbal, non-verbal); understand five love languages for friends and loved ones; celebrate key occasions; plan "dates"; engage in loved one's favorite activities; do three random acts of kindness weekly; donate blood; visit people in hospitals/nursing homes/senior centers; become a mentor

Leadership	Take leadership roles on projects/committees; organize multi-generational family event; organize community-wide event/block party/community yard sale/clean up; coach Little League/Girl Scouts
Humor	Learn one or two new jokes a week (and tell them); watch comedy channel/read comics daily; send funny emails (or post funny stuff); make a snowman (with kids even better); dress up for Halloween; do stand-up comedy
Sense of Community	Pick up litter; volunteer weekly for community service projects; attend community social gatherings; play in teams sports league; start a book club; work in a community garden; volunteer - Big Brother/Big Sister/Habitat for Humanity/Meals on Wheels/Food Pantry; monitor elderly neighbors; welcome new neighbors; join organization working with under-privileged; volunteer to educate; campaign on equal rights/human rights

HOW-TO COOL TOOL – Possibilities List if Work is in your Vision

Possibility lists if you are thinking about:

o Career Continuer – (extending your current business con-nections) - a new full-time or part-time job in same field of expertise, leading a professional association, looking at board membership, becoming editor of a journal in your field of expertise, freelancing or teaching in area of expertise, consultant, adjunct professor, online instructor, recruiter, speaker, corporate trainer, create and sell digital downloads/training

o Encore Career – consider starting your own business, return to college for new degree, retraining and licensing for new trade, open a B&B, get a real estate license, become a life coach/minister/financial advisor; be an independent sales consultant (franchise)

o   Part-time work in area of interest/hobby area (turning a lifelong passion/hobby into income generation) - consider monetizing a blog, working in store in area of interest (ex. fashion, home improvement, cooking, home decor); working in garden center at peak times; selling own crafts at local shows; performer (musician, actor, comedian)

o   Part-time job where time = money: freelance writing, photographer, seasonal work (summer camps, parks, stores), driving for Uber

o   Create a Small Business for day-to-day needs/services – dog walker, organizer, personal shopper, tax preparer, personal concierge, personal chef, business support services, home stager, proofreader, website developer, home companion, fitness instructor/personal trainer, professional e-Bay buyer/seller

o   New Skills/Certifications – mediator, teacher, healthcare worker/practitioner, realtor, minister, financial advisor, lawyer, become professional caretaker, tour director, adventure tour guide

Look at other people's lists! Steal and reapply. What does it spark for you? Does something make you say "Wow, isn't that cool?"

REAL LIFE EXAMPLE: When I add things to my Personal Possibilities List, I often will bold or star the ideas that are really inspiring to me. Below are some of those ideas; many of these became items on my action plan exploration early in my retirement.

Also when you look at your list, combinations of ideas will spark even bigger action plan ideas. Here's a real example: love of planning trips + wildlife spotting + luxury vacation + cross the equator + visit new countries + hot air balloon ride = a three-week African Safari trip with multiple mini-adventures for our twenty-fifth anniversary.

Start an exercise program	Visit new countries – goal fifty total	Super luxury vacation
Try yoga	Write a blog	Take writing class
Learn about birds	Big trip planning – 1/year	Consulting LLC
Become Life Coach	Visit all fifty-seven National Parks	Study mysticism
Create strong friend network	Improve social media skills	Get regular massage
Take cooking classes	Improve bicycling and take long trip	Cross the equator
Join a (new) church	Wildlife spotting	Walk the dog daily
Go to Craft Fairs	Hot Air Balloon	Join Foodie Club
See the Northern Lights	Explore RoadScholar/OLLI	Antique Dealer

YOUR IMAGINE SUMMARY

At this point you should:

- o Have a LONG LIST of ideas. . . hundreds of ideas!
- o Highlight some that really connect with your heartstrings.

It is okay if you need to go back to Reflect! Did you learn something new about yourself? Do you want to refine your vision statement?

CHAPTER 12

MAKING CHOICES
ASSESS PHASE

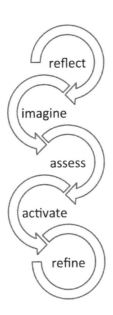

"It is not enough to be busy. . .what are you busy about?"
Thoreau

<u>MAKING CHOICES</u>

At this point in your retirement transition innovation process, it's about <u>intentionally choosing</u> the activities that will lead you down the path towards your vision. You need to become your own Life Curator.

The ASSESS phase is about choosing activities that will match the vision of life you created, which should link to your life meaning and satisfaction. You want to focus energy on the important few instead of the insignificant many.

Choose your life path . . . choose it on purpose.

Research indicates happy retirees have three to five core pursuits/interests with ten or more fulfilling activities. At this stage, some of your choices will be EXPLORATION. So you might not have nailed down your three to five core things.

You might be moving from a corporate-single-job mindset to a portfolio lifestyle of an artist. The arts community is used to several side businesses to make a living – from performing, editing, creating, and training in their artistic field while also boosting income with retail, serving, etc.

Do not stay busy just for the sake of busy. We live in a cult of busyness, but busy does not mean high performance or high satisfaction. Busy does not necessarily mean you are moving towards your vision. Busy does not give you time to see opportunities that emerge.

Does the knowing make the doing any easier? No. It's easy to think, speculate, and even theoretically plan. The Doing is more difficult. Make choices so you can move forward to ACTIVATE them.

Review your vision statement. Thinking again about your values from REFLECT – what are the MOST important areas to you within the Life Domains? These top domain elements (three or four) will become the starting "foundational framework" of your Action Plan.

Some things to consider:

o   What is the ideal lifestyle for percent time alone versus percent time with others (who specifically, what activities); how was this handled in the "me, you, we" conversation?

o   What about percent active versus non-active pursuits (what specifically, with whom). Don't assume either is better! Active means lots of things to do, high physical engagement,

116

and multi-sensorial. Non-active is slower paced, more scholarly pursuits, and more intellectual. Both are good.

o   Which activities will replace important benefits "work" met and you identified as benefits still needed?

o   What is my comfort level for risk? Do I need things to be more secure (routine, safe and responsible) or am I willing to take chances (new and different, adventure, pushing the envelope)?

o   What amount of time do I want to be devoted to different life domains?

REAL LIFE EXAMPLES: Many folks shorten their life domain choices to a shorthand pie-chart language. Some plans I've heard referenced:

- 30/30/30 – 30% time get to paid (work), 30% time to give back (volunteer), 30% time to goof off (hobbies)
- 30/30/30 or 3 F's – 30% for funds (work two or three days a week), 30% for family (grandkids), and 30% for fun
- 25/25/25/25 - 4 F's - fitness, fun, friends, funds
- 30/30/30 – creativity, service, adventure
- 50/50 – fitness (healthy living) and fun (travel, friends, theater, cards)

So Many Possibilities, Not Enough Time - How to choose?

When you consider all the potential things you can do on your Possibilities List – from experiences to try, classes to take, places to visit – the abundance of possibilities can actually lead to paralysis! Assessment and choice is hard work. And as I was advised: Only you can do the work to make choices because no one knows your foundational elements and life vision better than you.

Much of life-before-retirement was dictated by others' demands and schedules, from parents to teachers to bosses. Now you can choose the kind of days you want to live. Oh, the freedom. . . . and the stress!

"The way to simplicity lies through complexity."
Chinese proverb

Recall the Happiness By Design? You want to choose activities that will match the life vision you created – which is linked to your core values, building on your strengths and matching your interests.

o   Recall activities that are linked to interests that provide enjoyment, fun, and comfort.
o   Activities that are linked to interests and strengths/ skills provide challenge, engagement, and feelings of accomplishment.
o   Activities that are linked to core values, as well as interests and strengths/skills, provide a higher level of satisfaction and meaning.

HOW-TO COOL TOOL – CHOICE ASSESSMENT

Here is a tool I have found useful in assessing different possible activities/pursuits versus Life Vision Statement and Life Domain Components. Activities can impact multiple life domains, some positively (+) and some negatively (-). You want to have a mix of activities that more positively impact across life domains.

	Activity Idea:	Activity Idea:	Activity Idea:	Activity Idea:	Activity Idea:
Overall Vision Statement					
Domain Statement 1					
Domain Statement 2					
Domain Statement 3					

You can add in as many columns as you want! This is about linking your day-to-day activities to your life vision and life domains.

REAL LIFE EXAMPLE: Here is a shortened example of a Choice Assessment - looking at my Life Domains (with reference to my core values, strengths, interests) and a few ideas from my Personal Possibilities List:

	Activity Idea: Zumba Class	Activity Idea: Foodie Dinner Club	Activity Idea: Writing this book	Activity Idea: RoadScholar Travel
Overall Vision Statement	++	++	+	+
Fitness - Be Active (Value + Interest)	++	-	-	
Connections with Friends (Value)	+	++	-	
Work – Share Expertise (Value + Strength)	-	-	++	+
Leisure – Release the Artist Within (Interest)		+	+	

Working through this choice assessment (which was a much larger spreadsheet), I was feeling a sense of an abundance of possibilities and a lack of direction! Intentionally choosing the activities that will lead down the path towards my vision was not easy. A friend of mine commented at her four-month post-retirement mark: "Today my life is 30% volunteer stuff, 30% learning, and 30% family. And I am happy with that!" She got there much quicker than I did.

A few other suggestions about choosing activities/pursuits:

- <u>Focus energy on the important few instead of the insignificant many.</u> This is more than creating a full calendar (filling up time); it is about engaging in things that can bring life satisfaction. Busy-ness for the sake of busy-ness was a habit I had to break. In today's culture, busy-ness is the key sign of a workaholic and is also a signal of high performance. To say that you are "not busy" is a negative statement – a sign of laziness or even a signal that you need help – someone will definitely try to solve your non-busy problem with suggestions on things to do! But, busy can also mean being stressed and not being mindful, not doing what is really important to you, and not having time to think or watch for serendipity. I learned that a balance of the few scheduled, structured activities and some un-structured time allows me to feel not stressed, and not bored.

- <u>Definitely pick a couple of new things to just explore!</u> What about trying one new thing per season? You will be more dis-appointed by the things you did NOT try than the things you did! This is not about making a lifetime commitment. Try it on and if you don't like it (after giving it a real chance, don't be too discomforted with non-proficiency), move on and try something else. If the interest in the new thing is igniting, keep doing it. My writing class turned into a blog!

- <u>Talk with people about your plans.</u> When I mentioned plans to be more active with walking, I found a couple of walking com-panions (physical wellbeing AND connections to friends!). A friend recently asked me if I had done a "walk-about." He said to explore new possibilities by creating a list of people to talk to, organizations to connect with, classes to take, and places to visit for inspiration. I was encouraged to visit museums, talk to directors of arts organizations, link into volunteer boards on start-ups. All of this puts you "out there" to allow for seren-dipity to happen. . .almost planned serendipity.

- <u>Break it down.</u> As you look at big activity areas or big life domains, think about breaking them down. My Writing a Book (big activity) started with taking creative writing classes and starting to write a blog. Improve Physical Wellbeing (big domain) started with the goals of doing weekly Zumba and walking.

I relook at my activities/pursuits on a quarterly basis to see if they continue to stay aligned with my Life Vision, if overall I remain in balance (more play than work, not too much structure), if I need to stop doing something (it's not bringing me satisfaction), and if there is space for trying something new from my Life Possibilities List. We'll explore this more in REFINE.

ASSESS SUMMARY:

The Assess Phase is about comparing possibilities back to your core foundational understanding. At this point you should have:

o   Identified key Life Domains and some actions/activities that align with Life Vision.
o   Made initial choices on some activities/actions to pursue, including understanding the portion of your future that is "traditional work."
o   Thought through some me/you/we challenges.

It is okay if you need to go back to Reflect!

Did you learn something new about yourself?

Do you want to refine your vision statement?

Did you get more ideas to add to your Imagine list?

CHAPTER 13

ACTIVATE THE PLAN
ACTIVATE PHASE

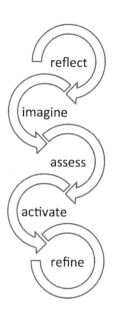

ACTIVATE: BEGIN THE EXPLORATION

This phase is about creating the Lifestyle that Expresses the Who You Want to Be. By design or by default, your next life stage will happen. Activating is taking control to explore restructuring life, experimenting with new activities, setting goals, and changing habits.

"Twenty years from now you will be more disappointed by the things you didn't do than the ones you did do. So throw off the bowlines. Sail away from safe harbor. Catch the trade winds on your sail. Explore. Dream. Discover."
Mark Twain

Activating is crafting the FIRST TRANSITION ACTION PLAN – and then experimenting and researching to implement your Life Vision - the WHO you want to be. If you don't activate, time just escapes, and the things you've envisioned will fade away.

With the specific activities chosen in ASSESS, activating is about:

- Getting clear on goals and measures: what is it I am trying to achieve and how will I know that I've gotten there?
- Re-setting or restructuring your world – finding a new day-to-day rhythm of life. Like me, you might be coming off thirty-plus years of full-speed working days, with hour after hour of meetings and email and reading and report writing. Re-setting a day-to-day "inner rhythm" as well as day-to-day routine will be critical.
- Understanding what your barriers are to implementing the plan.

As I know from many years in R&D, good creation takes time – It is about experimenting and prototyping, which is also often called trial and error. Because the "errors" help you learn about the things that do not work for you.

It is often easier to think, speculate, and plan than it is to do. Let's look at best practices in goal setting and how you might need to identify the inner voice or belief systems that is sabotaging you from taking action.

<u>**Learning Moment** – **Take Your Time**</u>

It is okay to take time on this. . . even if my Type-A personality is clamoring for the FULL Plan to be in place NOW. I've read/been told it can take up to three years for your new life plan to come together in retirement. And actually that you should not do anything right away! If you've spent time before retirement doing the self-reflection, then you might be ready to execute. But don't feel pressured. Self-discovery takes time.

Some take that "trip of a lifetime" the first year, or move to their retirement destination, or build their dream house. But I learned a term recently – "halfback." Halfbacks are people from Ohio who moved to Florida immediately as a retirement destination and then found it was not right. . . too hot! And then had to move again halfway back to North Carolina/Tennessee!

<u>Best Practices In Goal Setting:</u>

It is critical to set goals for chosen activity areas, even if they are about exploring or learning. Definitely include explore in your action plans! Pick a few things to "try on," to prototype, or experiment with. Give yourself permission to try and to nurture the activity to see if it grows.

- Write the goals down. When goals are written down, we automatically and unconsciously scan the environment for people and situations to facilitate their achievement. Refer to your goals regularly. Put activities on daily to-do lists that support your goals.
- Write goals in the positive end state. Doing something, not avoiding something. Create a visual of them. See yourself in the future state. . . living the activities you've identified, experiencing the who you see yourself being, living in the environment you set in your future vision.
- Make goals specific and measurable. What is it I am trying to achieve and how will I know that I've gotten there? Be clear on what it is. So instead of "I want to be more active," try "I am going to

walk 30 minutes a day a minimum of 3 times a week," "I am going to add strength training 2 times per week. . . in the morning while watching the GMA show!" Ranges are also good. . . for example: write 2-5 pages in a journal 5 times a week, or lose 5-10 pounds by Christmas by being more active.

- Think about the different types of goals possible – different levels like become an expert, become proficient, gain knowledge and enjoy, participate in and enjoy, etc. Separate learning goals from performance goals. For example: Learning is "take a creative writing class"; Performance is "complete writing the book." A learning goal can be just trying something new each month.

- Make them challenging but also achievable! Break down a big goal into sub-goals. For example, in learning a new skill: research classes, take the chosen class, and then implement a performance goal. Another example: plan to write three or four pages a week in my journal as inspiration for writing, and then transfer one idea to the computer a month for a blog post.

- Reward yourself or celebrate your success. If you need to feel a sense of accomplishment, keep a daily success journal with daily triumphs that include the little things – watching the sunset (as part of relaxation goal) or playing ball with the dog (part of be active goal). Celebrate accomplishing sub-goals along the way. This can also help create a reward structure for a new habit formation!

- Look for accountability partners. Share goals with others, if you feel comfortable. They will help you achieve them. When I told an "old friend" some of my goal areas, she reached out to me as she had similar goals and now we have a "regular date" for each of us to work on one of our common goals together. "Serendipity happens."

- Make sure they are under your control through your own efforts. But also be bold! Adopt the mantra: "I am brave enough to write down my goals/dreams and go after them. I am strong enough to deal with the fact that I might not achieve them all. The journey to try them is the fun part."

- Make sure this is still FUN. If it's not, re-evaluate the activity, the goal.

Barrier Busting

Does the knowing make the doing any easier? Sometimes things just can't get started! It's important to understand your "personal barriers" to change and how you might break through them.

When was the last time you truly changed a life pattern? Stopped a long-term habit? Started a new habit, formed a new relationship, or learned a new skill? Changing patterns is not easy – and a huge change like retirement transition doesn't make creating new habits a simple task. You do not wake up the day after you retired and become someone else overnight! You will have the same "habit-formation barriers" that you always had. You will have the same self-limiting voices telling you why you can't do something. By understanding what is stopping you - your own personal brick walls and fantasy fears - you can take small steps to break through them.

Our thoughts are either handcuffs or springboards; it's time to take off the handcuffs.

Barriers – We've got a Name for That

Reading through different people's transition blogs and talking with retirees, I've concluded that retirement transition is an amazingly individual transition. Because you're figuring out what you want to do next, it is all about you. It is nobody else's "should"! But I've also realized, there are some barriers that many people feel. And knowing you're not alone in the feeling can be helpful.

If the feeling has been "named," it indicates other people recognize what you are feeling. Feelings are not rational. They are the emotional elements within us; the facts are secondary, or even not involved many times! So it's nice sometimes to know you're not alone in the irrationality of feelings.

So here are some common barriers to change. They are not restricted to retirement transition, but they create unique challenges in this life stage. Some of these names are well known, but it's nice to acknowledge that other recent retirees are dealing with them, too.

- **The Bag Lady Syndrome** - This seems to occur among women of a certain age. First, we feel like we will never have enough money to retire. After retirement, we worry the money will not last through our retirement. We worry about being a Bag Lady. How much is enough? It's very often not about the numbers, but rather emotional confidence. It can prevent us from spending that hard-earned money on doing the things we always wanted to do – a barrier to living the life we want to have. It's critical to re-evaluate your finances, with a trusted advisor perhaps, to ground yourself in reality, not fantasy.

- **<u>The Imposter Complex</u>** - It is amazing how many smart, accomplished individuals dread being exposed as incompetent. An inner voice saying, "I'm not good enough," is so common! And in retirement transition, when you need to learn new things or create new habits, it can be a huge barrier to starting something. What if I put my heart and soul into this activity and nobody thinks it's any good? Trying new things where you are not the expert and things are not immediately done with mastery can quickly confirm this barrier! How to deal with an Imposter Syndrome?
    - o Start small. Start with something close to your comfort zone. And then allow the momentum to start. I started first trying things just slightly out of my comfort zone and then used that success (I did it!) to try something new further out of my comfort zone.
    - o Redefine failure. Don't "expect to be the expert" immediately, which is really setting goals too high. After being the expert at work for years, it is really hard to be a beginner. Mark Twain's quote is ubiquitous in retirement books: "Twenty years from now you will be more disappointed by the things you didn't do than the ones you did do." Define success as trying it. Or simply challenge the failure potential. So what if I fail? What is the worst thing that can happen if I try something and it doesn't work out? I needed to really internalize it – I will be more disappointed by the things I did NOT try than the things I did. I changed my sense of accomplishment to "I did it" versus a critique on the quality of the output.
    - o Give yourself permission to try. Pick a few new things to just explore. This is not about making a lifetime commitment!

Convince the inner voice telling you "you're not good enough" that you are only exploring the possibility or taking a single class "just to see." Remember, doing something well takes patience, determination, and follow through. If the excitement in the activity is igniting, then you can think about putting in the 10,000 hours to become the expert. And, it is okay to stop something if you don't like it or if it is not making you happy. Nurture the activity to see if it grows. . . if not, move onto something else on the list.

o "Believe in yourself" affirmations can help. "I am good enough. My life successes to date were a result of my talents and hard work and dedication and can be reapplied to my future choices." Another simple Barrier Buster Affirmation: "It's OK to be a beginner."

Realize, so what if you are not perfect at it. . . more people will be impressed that you TRIED it! Yes, they will be! They will be totally impressed you went as a single to a Food & Wine event. They will be totally impressed you are taking drawing classes (one blogger friend is, and it's amazing), taking ballroom dance classes, or writing a blog (okay, some people will be impressed and yes, they will tell you!). Build on the positive "impressed" feedback you hear and try something else.

- **Analysis Paralysis.** Are there so many possibilities on the list that you just can't start anything? I've heard this one more than once as well! What if I choose wrong? Some barrier-busting tools to use:
   o Make choices between possibilities based on the activity's fit with your personal values-based vision. Use the Choice Assessment worksheet.
   o Realize most things do not need to be a long-term commitment! Try something for a class series, a month, or a season.
   o Be careful to not take on too many activities – be okay with consciously putting things on hold (like finding a local yoga class) as you try on something else (writing class). You can try something else next month, next season. Everything does not need to be done immediately.

- o   Think through: I am really trying to choose things because they are MY choices. Any time I hear the word "should" (You should be working part-time in retirement. . . three days a week is the goal.), it puts up a warning sign for me.

- **The Inner Critic** - Be aware of limiting, negative self-talk. The Inner Critic can be very vocal and judgmental in a number of ways: "You're no good at stuff like that. You're too fat, too old, too out of shape, too stupid. Who do you think you are? Nobody in their right mind does that." Silencing the voice is tough, so I have found that:
  - o   Find a cheerleader. When I recently told a friend that I didn't think I could do one of my possibilities, she just squashed my negativity, "Of course you can do that. I can see you totally doing that."
  - o   Have a conversation with that voice and do a reality check. Okay, it sounds a little weird, but the "voice of failure" is usually not based on the reality of your life. Sometimes a look back at your past accomplishments can get that voice to be quiet. Say to that voice: "You're wrong, look at this accomplishment."
  - o   Follow the voice's path and have a conversation: So what if I try this? What will happen? Okay, now bring some logic in – what REALLY will happen? As my husband said when I was scared about learning to stand-up paddleboard, "You fall in, you'll get wet, so what?"
  - o   Let go of the fantasy fears with affirmations. As Nike says, "Just Do It." Mine went as follows: You ARE a smart, competent, capable woman, just exploring something new and fun. Trying something is the accomplishment. It doesn't need to be perfect; you don't need to be the expert. You will be happier to have tried it, and others will be so impressed you did as well!

- **The Good Girl Handcuffs** - This could also be called, "I want to stop living the 'should.'" So many of us grew up on the "should." I should be the good girl and not fight with my siblings. I should study hard and get good grades. I should graduate with honors and get a well-paying job. I should work hard, adjust to the company work style, and climb the corporate ladder. I should be a feminist and a role model to other women. In many ways, I've done the "should" my whole life. Being the good girl, I have abided by most of society's expectations. Now the "shoulds" are my handcuffs. How can I stop being the good girl - doing the expected things, the pleasing others thing?

Built-in here is also the **Comparative Inferiority Complex**, which are all the thoughts that someone else is doing it better. I should be working a second career (like they are), should be volunteering (like they are), should be traveling (like they are), should be exercising every day (like they are), or should be busier than ever (like they are). Should, should, should. What if I'm not working, not giving back, not traveling, or not exercising every day? What if I am not busy?

Even many of the articles written about retirement will support the "should." They have the arguments for why you should be focusing on giving back to bring life satisfaction. And why you should exercise every day for longevity. And data to support being busy as linked to happiness. In today's society, busy is a sign of achievement and importance. It's just not socially acceptable to not be busy.

Also builit in here is the "I feel guilty not working!" Yes, I never realized how strong my own Puritan Work Ethic is! When people comment: "What do you mean, you're NOT working?" If you're not working, you are obviously lazy, a sloth, morally weak, a drain on society, going to vegetate on a couch and die an early death. Yes, sloth is one of the seven deadly sins! I am definitely not being the "good girl" I was raised to be. And the Bag Lady worry of "Do I have enough money?" builds this guilt higher.

In retirement transition, you want to break free of the "should," the comparison to others. Stop trying to meet everyone else's expectations of what they think is best for you, or what you think they think because that's what they are doing.

- o Re-clarify your personal values! When you have linked your activities to your value-based life vision, you can more easily say, "Good for you, but it's not for me."
- o Translate the Compare and Despair (I'm not and I should) to Compare and Empower. Give them positive feedback for what they are accomplishing – it might be an out-of-comfort-zone thing for them. Be their cheerleader! Use their accomplishment as inspiration, if the activity fits within your own life vision. "If they can do it, so can I."
- o And as one friend keeps telling me: "Just stop should-ing on yourself."

- **The Someday Habit** - This one is especially common among workaholics and/or early retirees. You got in the habit of putting off things – to save the money for retirement. So many things are in the camp of delayed gratification – the places to go, things to learn, activities to try. "I'll do it someday." Now it's a habit, and long-held habits, ones you've had for years, are hard to break. How can you move from someday to just-do-it now?

  A subset of the someday habit is a lack of "activation energy"! The complete opposite of Nike's "Just do it" is "I just can't get started!" Have you always had a tendency to procrastinate? Are you letting the easy couch-dom living to become your total reality? Are non-productive, mindless activities (watching TV for hours, endless Internet surfing, blog black holes) taking over your life?

  Breaking the someday habit and boosting your activation energy comes from reaffirming what you've envisioned in your life plan and doing some intentional planning. (If you are naturally a spontaneous person, you're probably not dealing with a someday habit!)

o Simply ask: What am I waiting for? Use affirmations: Someday is here. Now is the time. Consider challenging yourself: How will I feel in five years if I don't do this?

o Try to determine if the things you've been "putting off" are truly things you want to do now. Am I willing to work, put in the time and effort, towards making this a reality? Will I enjoy the process of learning that new skill, achieving that goal? Or does the learning process look to be more like frustration? If I'm not willing to work at it, then I just need to acknowledge it is a fantasy and will never be reality. Drop it from the list.

o Break down the activity into manageable elements. Start with a small step. Put that step on the calendar and treat the item on your calendar as a personal commitment. Yes, I have put time on my calendar to "find the class online and book it" or "edit one chapter of your book." Movement breeds movement.

o Take a deep breath and sign up for a course or class. This can be viewed as a commitment to the teacher to show up. Or the "If I pay for it, I am more likely to do it."

o Link something you want to start to another activity, which helps with forming a new habit. So I linked my morning journal writing to my morning cup of coffee habit.

o Find a buddy or a support system – someone with a similar interest, a similar dream. I found a walking companion and got a foodie club started with a few acquaintances. We are in it together now.

o Verbalize it (what you want to do someday) and allow serendipity to work for you. By talking to others about my retirement journey or what they found interesting/helpful on their journey, I learned about a local cooking school boot-camp (someday I'll take a serious cooking class) and linked with a past colleague who wants to partner on some white-papers (someday I'll be a real writer). Another friend regularly asks me how my travel planning is going.

To identify my own personal barriers, I needed to listen to what my inner critic was saying. And think about what stopped me from making a change in the past. What prevented me from trying something new, or stopping some old, non-positive habits? Why was I waiting for the perfect alignment of things? Why was I allowing non-productive, mindless activities to come before the things I envisioned about doing? I realized that the implementation of my vision started with some small steps. And nothing needed to be perfect. I began with daily/weekly goals that moved me towards my vision, and a lot of affirmations.

HOW-TO COOL TOOL – Affirmations

Consider what positive affirmations can help break your own personal barriers. Here are some you might pick and chose from. Or create your own!

o   Someday is today!
o   It's OK to be a beginner.
o   I am enough – smart enough, capable enough.
o   Sometimes it's okay to just be. Not do. Just be.
o   It's a good (enough) plan for now.
o   I am being the me I envision myself to be.
o   I am right where I need to be on life's journey.
o   I find joy in today. I do something (small) every day that I love to do.
o   I am spending time on things that I value. I do things I want to do, not should do.
o   Today, I will just put something new or something just for fun on the calendar and do it.
o   I will be joyfully creative, and not worry about how good the output is.
o   I recognize that I am not willing to put in the effort to lose weight, but I will plan activities with friends that are not always passive or food-centric.

When you are the concierge of your own life, everything that comes onto your calendar is delightfully by your own choice. But that also means everything that comes onto your calendar, you have to put

133

there! No more project/team/budget meetings regularly pre-scheduled. No more requests from mentees for lunch dates/coffee dates or a half hour of time to talk about an issue. Every week, every day, every minute is yours to decide how to fill. This is both freeing and daunting.

Nurture a new activity to see if it grows. If not, move onto something else on the list. If it does grow into something you love, awesome. This could be your passion (or one of them) you can grow into a "life calling."

Balance of Be-ing and Do-ing

A lot of what we've been exploring is about doing, activities, pursuits, and goals. So is it more important to do or to be? As in most of life, it's a balance. For me, the easier was the "do." So the learning was in the "be."

Part of my retirement transition has been an exploration into happiness. There are many hypotheses about what drives happiness, especially later in life, but ones that seem to have conflicting messages are the concepts of be-ing and do-ing. Some of the retirement gurus claim that doing multiple activities results in more happiness. Other gurus claim that being, not doing, brings happiness. And of course, both have their own data and studies to prove it!

A quote from Dale Carnegie completely captures the importance of do-ing:

> *"Inaction breeds doubt and fear.*
> *Action breeds confidence and courage.*
> *If you want to conquer fear,*
> *do not sit home and think about it.*
> *Go out and get busy."*

On be-ing, there is the idea of finding the joy in being non-productive. Being in the moment. Finding the stillness and mindfulness of quiet time. Be okay with not having constant activity. Of course, for a recovering workaholic, this is a daunting concept. Just being? Isn't this just wasted time?

On the do-ing, there is the idea that a successful retirement is doing what I want, when I want, with whom I want. Choosing things that truly fit with your life vision – not the ones you think you should be doing. And in the doing, you find your true sense of purpose. Have the action plans and the checklists. Try out the new activities, get off the couch every day, and be active.

As a recovering workaholic, getting busy and doing the work is a theme in many quotes I seem to gravitate towards:

- "There is no Fairy Godmother. If you want to change your life for the better, you need to do the work."
- "Don't let fear drive procrastination. Take action; do something; do anything. What are you waiting for?"
- "You need to work through the complexity to find the simplicity."

But, I have come to the point of view that everyone does need to allow time for the moments to "be." Slow down and enjoy. . . the sunset, the thunderstorm, the star-filled night sky, the butterfly landing on flowers, or the smell of the roses (yes, I could smell them on my porch the summer while I was writing this book – I never knew that before!). Leave time in your schedule to act upon the chance opportunities – the stopover for grill out or have an extra ticket call from a friend, the see it in the paper weekend event, the whatever. Stop and listen to people, have the conversation – with your spouse, with a neighbor, with the retail person.

For many, finding joy in "non-productive" days is a learning curve. I personally got a coffee mug that said: "Find joy in each day," to remind myself to be more mindful and in the moment – just being.

Some other aspects to help with be-ing (not do-ing):

- Savoring the slowness, the stillness. Being okay with just sitting and watching the waves on the beach. Stopping for a coffee or a drink and just sitting. Watching the birds in the tress or the clouds in the sky.
- Enjoying having a less rigid schedule. Be okay to move a task to tomorrow, or the next day if something else comes up.

- Only checking email and FB once (okay, twice) a day. Not every hour. Get out of the rat-race. Maybe even do a full day (weekend) off grid!
- Enjoying the little things – browsing through a store for the joy of browsing, reading a book for the joy of reading, strolling through the neighborhood.
- And importantly, know it is okay to have "do nothing time" on your calendar!

BLOG POST: Learning the joy of an empty calendar

Busy is a sign of worthiness, a sign of being needed and wanted, a sign of achievement and success. I found that a completely empty calendar just made me feel worthless, adrift, and unhappy.

When I have multiple days in a row that are empty, negative emotions start to arise. . . a feeling of the blahs, doubt about this life plan, worry that I'll become one of the retirement bad case studies – you know, the one who "gave up on life and died just two years after retirement." Yes, I use my tools (gratitude, reading others inspirational blogs, etc.) to pull myself up. But the root cause? I have come to the realization that I need to be a better planner.

To keep the blahs at bay, I need a daily schedule. It's a balance between loving the freedom of not having to do or be anywhere on a regular basis and yet still having something to do or someplace to be almost every day.

There is a lot of retiree sentiment that I 'should' enjoy a non-scheduled life. Stop and smell the roses, watch the grass grow, enjoy the sunset. Would I feel better if I scheduled that in?

When I look over the broader time frame, it's easy to see the answer to "What do you spend your time doing?" The big picture – a feast! I have a small, but regularly scheduled exercise program. I have friend connects, my "playing with words" activities, some out and about activities, and my consulting project work. I regularly look for opportunities. So when I have multiple days of nothingness (the famine days), I know it's just my own fault for not planning something.

I don't want a fairy godmother to create a dress for the ball; I want a fairy godmother to be my personal life-concierge. . . one who knows me as well as I know myself and makes the plans to avoid the "famine days."

Then there was the flip side of busy-ness. Am I hiding behind the to-do list? I'm busy; therefore, I am important and valuable. I'm busy; therefore, I'm worthy. I'm busy, so I don't need to look carefully at what my life is or isn't? Am I hiding behind the busyness instead of doing the work to cultivate meaningful relationships or challenge myself with new experiences?

I learned:
* I need to find the right balance between structured-scheduled activities and go-with-the-flow freedom. Will I ever find joy in a completely empty calendar? No. But a couple days of freedom a week feels quite nice.
* I need to learn to slow down - find the positive in stillness, engage fully in the present, allow time for introspection, and surrender to serendipity. Look at an empty calendar as an opportunity to savor the slowness.
* I need to watch out on freedom days - not allow passive time-wasters to take over that free time. Don't let free time turn into mindless TV watching, blog surfing, and the FB black hole.
* I need to challenge myself on what the activities are that make the schedule. Scheduling activities and being busy is easy. Are the things I am busy doing making me happy? Stimulating my mind? Activating my vision?

Retirement does not need a checklist, but you might need one! Just remember to keep everything flexible and to allow for the spontaneity and joy of the moment or the last minute invitation you can say "yes" to.

Intention versus Behavior

Our attitudes and intentions do not equate to our actual habitual behavior! <u>Just stating an intention to change does not make it happen</u>. When I heard this researched fact, it was mind opening. So much about entering into retirement for many of us is about habit change – from creating new daily schedules to starting new hobbies to making healthy living changes in diet and exercise.

Habitual behaviors, even infrequent habits, allow us to function; we've essentially created habits to remove decision-making and simplify our lives. No one can make a decision about everything, every day – it would go beyond just cognitive fatigue. Existing behaviors/habits reduce risk – we know the outcome, they keep our lives in some sort of balance. Whether those habits are good for us or not, they are firmly ingrained. Changing a habit is risky – we don't know the outcome, and it could have an adverse effect. We might not even consciously realize our resistance.

To make a habit change, the focus needs to be on reducing the resistance to change. Some approaches to <u>increase odds of habit change</u> (reducing the resistance):

- Piggyback on an existing behavior/habit
- Make new behavior less painful/easier than current behavior
- Holistically "design" the new behavior, so it is visually and emotionally appealing
- Provide short-term rewards for behavior shift
- Improve perception of behavioral change outcomes – remove cognitive resistance

As I thought about my own retirement lifestyle desire for more healthy habits related to eating and exercise, I contemplated what strategies/actions might fit some of these approaches. It has to be more than just stating my intention to eat better and exercise more! Some I've implemented, some I need to re-energize, and some I need to plan conscious action around:

- Keep "good snacks" around and in sight – popcorn, fruit, cut veggies. Stop buying big bags of chips (and keep the chip bag hidden in the pantry).
- Keep buying those pre-packaged salads. . . yeah, they are more expensive, but they taste good, and I eat them!
- Always use my favorite, hand-made bowl to serve a snack (i.e., don't eat right out of the bag).
- Keep planning walks with friends, instead of lunches.
- Buy a multi-class yoga pass (again). I've already bought the cute yoga pants!
- Buy easy-to-prepare, good tasting foods for breakfast, so it's not just coffee for breakfast.
- Plan ahead some dinners each week and put them on the calendar; explore some new recipes – and enjoy my new kitchen!

What habit change can you apply these reducing resistance ideas to?

Learning Moment: AN ASIDE on De-Cluttering

Clutter is a nagging reminder of things undone, of choices not made. Stuff crowds your mind, your environment, and your life. Freeing up space allows your new self to grow, figuratively and physically. Retirement Transition is a perfect time to think about: What is cluttering up your physical space? What is cluttering up your emotional space? Do you need physical space to start a new hobby? Does the kitchen need de-cluttering to encourage you to cook more or eat more healthily? Do you need to distance yourself from emotional energy drainers?

Stuff often feels like security – just in case, you never know when you might need that. Unfortunately, it is highly unlikely you will ever need that!

Stuff can trigger memories. But how often do you go through the boxes of pictures, pick up those books? Collected stuff is not living in the here and now.

It's okay to let go of stuff! We outgrow things; our tastes change. The physical object served its purpose in your life. . .it's okay to let it go now. Make the stuff in your life be important to the choices you are making now in implementing your life vision.

Some things that just need to go: old sports gear, work clothes you will never wear again, clothes that don't fit (if you lose that twenty-five pounds, buy yourself some new things to celebrate), old tech items, old books, artwork you no longer want to hang on the wall, kitchen things you never use (yes, that thing you've never used since you got it for your wedding). . . anything outdated, worn out, or never used. Donate it, toss it out, sell it. But get rid of it.

I love the concept of "salvaging" your wardrobe in retirement. What things can you re-position and wear in new ways? And really consider, how many black pants, suit jackets, or black pumps do you need going forward? Re-purpose or donate!

At the end, you want your "stuff "to be beautiful, useful and well-loved. . . . to fill your life with joy.

ACTIVATION SUMMARY

Don't let fears or old belief systems become permanent procrastinators. Give yourself permission to be a little bit afraid, but don't let the voices of negativity stop you. Don't expect perfection. You might be back to being a learner versus the expert. That is okay. Challenge yourself to get out of your comfort zone. . . you will feel a sense of accomplishment just by trying it.

You will not wake up the day after you retire and suddenly be a new person. You will have the same habit formation challenges you've always had. To make changes requires small steps every day to become the person you want to be.

Balance pre-set structure and time for serendipity, allowing space for spontaneity and just downtime. It's not just about checklists and busy schedules. Those are good to help in activating, but also take time to relax. Take time to decompress your body and your mind from years of working and find a new daily rhythm.

Think about: What are five small changes you can make in your life right now? Maybe it's setting aside personal time to do self-reflection, or identifying something that is a small step towards one of your big goals, or bringing a jolt of joy into your life. (I bought fine point blue pens!) Even a small, almost insignificant change can unleash a sense of personal power.

And, remember the power of affirmations.

CHAPTER 14

CONTINUAL RENEWAL
REFINE PHASE

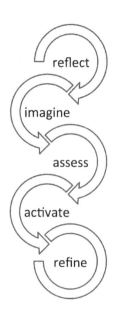

REFINE: CONTINUAL RENEWAL OF THE PLAN

Renew, revise, refresh, and rejuvenate. Moving from ninety-day plans to annual plans. Realign, modify, and adjust as needed.

"Go confidently in the direction of your dreams!
Live the life you've imagined."
Thoreau

You now have your vision of the future and a plan to have good days filled with satisfying activities. It's important to have the vision of the future, a direction to be heading. It's important to have a plan, a blueprint to build that future vision. These give you reasons to get up every day. Each day contributes in meaningful ways to the vision you have of your life as a whole.

Build day-by-day or week-by-week plans to implement your life vision. Many have found it easier to first put together a three-month plan, then another three-month plan, and then another three-month plan. This corresponds to the old work quarterly plans many are used to. Or the seasonal plans many prefer.

Consider a first-year plan that isn't about going towards Life Vision yet, but rather is more about working through this process. A first ninety-day plan could be about taking time for a break, decompressing your mind and your body, or finishing up big "honey-do lists" or going through and organizing things and preparing for the journey.

Then, review your plan quarterly, or bi-annually.

Does what you are doing and whom you are spending your time with reflect your vision? If the plan is working, if time is flying by and you have plenty of energy, if you look forward to starting every day, if you feel happy and fulfilled – then keep going!

But it is also absolutely okay, and sometimes necessary, to change things – to modify the Vision, to pick new Life Domains for focus, to change the Action Plans. Life happens. External factors can have a significant effect. Life circumstances can change. . . in so many ways.

A plan is only something in place from which you can deviate and modify! You are the boss; if your plan is not working, change it. **Your plan should never be written in stone** but should provide you a basic blueprint to return to, so you are actively creating the life you want.

In your daily/weekly activities plans, you need to find space for both vision-path activities and the life maintenance (sleep, shop and eat, pay bills, do laundry, yard work). Am I doing one thing every day that moves me towards my future vision? Am I becoming the person I want to be? Do I have a balance between scheduled activities and go-with-the-flow time to just "be"?

When doing a review, look at what activities you've added in should stay, and which should go. What is bringing you satisfaction? Is it creative pursuits, upcoming travel, household projects, daily exercise, conscious connections? Do you want to do even more of that?

What you learn about an activity that is satisfying, or not, can impact your plan going forward. If something disappointed, disillusioned or depressed you, eliminate it. If you find yourself excessively eating, sleeping, watching TV or feeling sorry for yourself, pull out your plan and re-evaluate it – does the vision still feel right?

What if you're just not happy? Give a good look at the activities where you are spending your time. Are they linked to your interests, strengths, and values? Are they linked to your life vision statement? Do you need to change the activities or rethink what really is important to you?

Make intentional choices and not just activity by default! Is there anything on my calendar that I'm doing, not because I want to or it's the right thing for my life/my family, but because it's expected of me? Or because I've invested a bunch of time/money/life pursuing that path and I don't want to admit failure/it's not working?

Explore your barriers, recommit to the goals, and kick-start your plan! Or revise it with new action elements and goals. Remember, habits take repetition to establish. Don't let one mis-step derail the whole journey. Restarting something (again and again if needed) is perfectly fine.

Go back to your Personal Possibilities List for new things to explore. What thing(s) would I really regret not checking off that I need to begin activating now? What on my Personal Possibilities List will bring me joy now? Why do some items on my Personal Possibilities List create a feeling of gut clenching? Is it just that the idea of trying it makes me feel incompetent and I really do want to try it? Or is it because they really do not match what's important?

Be open to new ideas to continue to fill your Possibilities List. Listen for opportunities, especially ones that fit your life vision! Refresh the plan as new opportunities come along.

REAL LIFE EXAMPLE: My first 90-day plan took an in-depth review of the finances to understand the big time points as well as monthly/yearly cash flows – moving 401Ks, stating distributions from IRAs, applying for Medicare, stock option dates, Social Security and pension start dates, and a new retirement lifestyle cash flow/budget.

My second 90-day plan had me focusing on an increased comfort with online social media from LinkedIn to Facebook to blogs to Pinterest and figuring out how to pay bills online. I also began exploring options for a regular exercise program.

After a while, I moved to quarterly plans that coincide with the seasons. I now often link to blog posts about seasonal bucket lists – putting my seasonal plans in the public eye for support and accountability. When I posted one season that I wanted to try ten new restaurants that quarter (a mini-adventure), I had many volunteers to help me achieve that goal!

HOW-TO COOL TOOL – Activities vs Values Assessment

Kegan's work on adult development states that achieving Stage 4 (higher order adult development) means your personal actions/behaviors (what you actually do) are aligned with your values. So understanding your personal values and beliefs in relationship to your activities can help improve your emotional health.

This assessment tool is a great way of exploring if what you are doing is linked to what's really important. Essentially, can you fill in the statement, "I value x, so I spend my time, energy and money on a, b, c," and have it make sense?

In the assessment chart, you attempt to link both your values to your Vision Statement, the Vision Statement to your action plans or goals, and then the reality of where you actually do spend your time. It can be filled in forwards or backwards, and I encourage you to use both directions! And make sure that you list of all your activities across the week/month/quarter.

Value (X)	What I want to be/do (vision statement)	What I planned	What I actually do – how I spend my time and energy (a,b,c,)

As you filled in the chart, do not be surprised if there are some rows where you had time spent (things I actually do), but not any link to a value. Are these time wasters? Or possibly a miss in your values articulation and you need to clarify your real values? Are you doing things that are "should" versus your real values?

You might also see misses in your vision statement versus plans. Are there activities you needed to add into your plans, or are you intentionally delaying that part of the Vision? Are the inconsistencies between planned actions and actually how you spend your time? Are your intentions (plans) not linked to actual behaviors? Is there a barrier you can identify here?

This is not a check-box tool, but a way to assess if your activities, behaviors, and daily rhythm are aligned to your core values.

REAL LIFE EXAMPLE: A few statements in the assessment approach were easy.

"I value x, so I spend my time, energy and money on a, b, c."

I value belonging and I want to be a good friend, so I spend my time creating and implementing intentional connections via blogging, setting up dinners with friends, and planning girlfriend Walk & Talks.

And I identified some gaps.

I value knowledge and I want to use my expertise to help others (and be recognized for that). I plan to become a certified retirement coach, write a blog, and the biggie – publish a book about retirement transition. But I found in the assessment I was continually putting off writing the book! I was spending a lot of computer time and energy playing games, looking at Facebook, or endlessly reading other people's blogs. I found I needed to get more intentional in the book writing, including exploring barriers that were keeping me not doing it!

BLOG POST: Start- Stop-Continue

Years ago, one of the MegaCorp annual performance evaluation tools we used was the "Start, Stop, Continue." I'm not sure how broadly this was used, but it was better than the "accomplishments and weaknesses" of previous years. That was before the Discover Your Strengths phenomenon (***StrengthsFinder*** by Tom Rath); I always hated the weaknesses area!

But the Start-Stop-Continue was brought back to my mind as I recently read a few articles about stopping things once you reach a certain age. As I approach my "annual review" of being retired, I realized that at this point in my life there are few things I do need to stop doing:

Stop comparing yourself to others. Banish the Comparison Inferiority habit. Between Facebook and blogs, I find myself often thinking, "Wow, she's doing that, why aren't I?" And the tone of that question is not in the positive, you-can-do-it manner. Rather the tone implies that I am, once again, comparing and lacking. I need to recognize that everything in social media is distorted – you only see a one-sided picture. I need to admire what she has done, and if it fits in my life vision, then choose to add it in and consciously build it into my life plan. Travel all over Asia, move into an RV, become a painter? Probably not. Become more active? Go out and about around town? Yes, that fits me and I can do that. Stop eating on autopilot. Besides being a self-professed foodie and a lover of good conversation over a meal, I am also an emotional eater.

I eat when I am frustrated or feeling insecure. I eat when I feel guilty about something. I eat when I don't know what else to do on a Sunday afternoon. I have not figured out how to stop this! I don't have the willpower to do the "not in the house" approach. I have at least tried to minimize it. I now have a small, beautiful snack bowl – the key word is *small.* No more single size packages of anything. I also buy healthy snacks, as well as the salty and sweet. So sometimes I am mindlessly munching on carrots instead of chips.

Stop dwelling on the past. I've written before about not living with regrets, but lately, I've started to wonder if I've missed out on some experiences. I never went to prom, never was in a sorority, never did the dating scene (bar hopping with the girls), never became a mom, and never had the close-couple friendships I see others have. (Yes, that last one was a Facebook comparison!) I know that the past is the past and I am where I am because of the choices I made. And where I am is a pretty awesome place. I need someone to remind me of that every so often!

It's the Journey

For many years, my husband has given me things (T-shirts, bumper stickers, magnets) with the iconic quote, "It's the journey, not the destination." He did it teasingly, because as a Type-A, goal-setting workaholic, I was always about the destination. In retirement, I am (slowly) coming to realize it IS about the journey. But the goal-setter achiever in me still needs to know, how do you measure the experience and not the endpoint? So here's how I measure the journey:

- First measure – Am I enjoying it? This is my life, so am I having fun living it? Is the activity I'm engaging in really what I want versus what I think I should be doing? The retirement "shoulds" can come from well-meaning individuals and/or long-term beliefs. There's even the research that says what retirement should include – a sense of purpose, volunteering, healthy living, supportive connections. I continue to sort through the "should" to my true desires - a challenge that continual self-discovery helps. Enjoying the activities I choose is a great measure of success along the journey.

- Second measure – Am I giving it my best shot? So many new things to try to determine if they fit in my journey– from daily journaling to taking classes to starting an exercise program with walking, Zumba and yoga. So am I giving each aspect a best shot to incorporate it into the journey? I am intentionally choosing to focus on fewer things, so I can put in the effort on new things.
- Third measure – Am I seeing my vision come to life? Having a vision, in both words and visuals, is important for me being the goal-setter. Regularly checking to see if my weekly activities are aligned with that vision gives me a regular measure of progress.

New Habits Take Time

Old habits take a long time to break. Comparative Inferiority (Compare and Despair) rears its head regularly. Getting depressed about an empty calendar. Not activating a long-held plan, and moving it once again to the next season's action plan. Movement not happening every day. A part of me wants more things "to do" and another part of me worries about overdoing and feeling even more overwhelmed. I can become the Queen of Wasting Time for days – iPad gaming, FB-ing, trash novel reading - because that gives me a sense of numbness.

I know what to do. I keep working the tools – small step goal setting, gratitude, affirmations, planning fun things, modifying the plan as needed. But over time I did notice:

- Intentionally replacing the effortless connections and support network of the workplace worked! I realized that the yearlong effort I put into setting up dates, calling people, arranging activities together, and commenting on blogs resulted in an abundance of friendships. Intentional investment of time and energy into maintaining these friendships remains an important part of my lifestyle vision.
- Coping with the loss of career identity meant I began doing consulting work projects and exploring life coaching. Work came so easy that I ended up returning to my workaholic tendencies. Not

good. This provided me a big wake-up call as to what I really wanted my retirement lifestyle to look like and a reset of the Action Plan.

- I explored new and engaging ways to stay active and be adventurous (for me). I realized I needed to identify activities and adventures that aligned with my conservative, mainstream, Midwest, structured personality! Many activities became new habits like writing a blog, doing yoga, Zumba, running a foodie club, and regular Walk & Talks with friends. I also planned and took the trip of a lifetime (three-week African safari). But quite a few things were tried and not continued. I'm still glad I tried them on!

- Removing things that no longer fit was a huge element as we changed our primary living situation. This involved defining what we both wanted in a new home, identifying the solution to a challenging family situation, and de-cluttering us. These activities were both mentally and physically challenging. I also faced a significant health crisis in the first few years, which again revised the plan.

HOW-TO COOL TOOL - Ten Lives

This is a great tool if you are trying to overcome fear with starting something or fear of committing to something long term.

Write down Ten Lives you would like to live. Look at your Personal Possibilities List or think about the activities you've selected to try on your Choise Assessment. Then, pick one thing you want to do and <u>do it for a month.</u> Just a one-month commitment!

REAL LIFE EXAMPLE: A Month of Yoga. I was given a yoga mat five years ago as a Christmas present from my husband when I mentioned I was interested in trying yoga. Yes, he listened, and yes, that was five years ago. So this has been on my Possibilities List for a long time. And yes, it fit under the "what are you waiting for?" conversation. I was also afraid of looking incompetent as a beginner – an "old" beginner whose body cannot do a lot of those yoga moves.

But the one-month commitment mindset gave me a feeling of "Okay, I can do anything for one month!" I bought a one-month pass and took a fifty-plus class to start. And went back to another class even though I felt completely uncomfortable in the first class. And then went back for a third – I had bought a full month and was not going to waste the money! My goal was to try three or four different classes a week.

So after a month of yoga, I decided to stick with it! My goal now is two classes a week. I'm more comfortable in class, but also know I need to find instructors who deal well with beginners as well as have a more "nurturing" personality. And I need to listen to my own body. I'm still very much a beginner, but even after two months of classes, I saw an improvement in my flexibility and strength.

BLOG POST: Invest in Friendship

There is a lot of research about the benefits of a strong circle of friends, especially as we grow older. It seems like all the research published is on why it's important, but little is ever written on how to do it! How do you maintain friendships? How do you establish friendships when traditional ways (school, work) are gone? The "how" type of information is harder to locate and was therefore precious when I did find it.

In retirement, I needed to move from the convenience and reliance on work for my casual, social connections to actually learn new ways to develop and maintain connections. I needed to learn the how – the "art of friendship."

William Rawlings, professor of Interpersonal Communication at Ohio University, stated: "Satisfying friendships need three things: somebody to talk to, someone to depend on, and someone to enjoy." He also points out two critical elements for developing friendship:

- Make the time and do it consistently; spending time together is critical to friendship formation. By intentionally investing in areas of your own interests, the three elements of quality friendship have a higher likelihood of being met.

- Listen when others share. Take the time to learn about them — not for them to learn about you. This is not about rebuttal or one-upmanship in conversation. When others feel listened to, they are more likely to feel positive to you.

An investment of time is required. Here's a few how-to invest in friendships tips I've found in various articles and tried to implement:

- Regular attendance at something. Church, yoga, an exercise class. Pick something and commit to attending for at least six to eight visits. And while there, talk to people! If someone expresses interest in you, then follow up with a one-on-one coffee date, or walking date, or something
- Find a club that matches your interests, whether it's a walking club, book club, writers' group, pickle-ball, or bird watching. Again, pick something and then regularly attend and talk with/listen to others. Meet-ups are a great way to locate groups of interest; or your local OLLI, senior center, YMCA, rec center.
- Plan something yourself, regularly, and invite others to join in. If people keep showing up, keep doing it.

The thing I noticed about all of these how-tos was the time investment needed -- the regularity of connection. In the past (school, work), that regularity of connection was simpler — it came with the job, or the kid's activities. Now, in retirement, those regular connections need to be created.

Learning the skill of listening is also quite challenging! With my storyteller traits, I noticed I'm often doing "one-upmanship" in conversation. Perhaps I was taught this was a way to establish connection. Now I need to learn to listen more, to be present in the conversation, and ask a question of their experience versus give my own experience.

It's also about giving of yourself. I've recently changed my thinking on planning activities. I've tried to move from frustration that I seem to always be the planner (old thinking) to thinking this is my gift to them. It's a bit of selfish pay-it-forward -- they enjoy the activity, but I do, too!

Investing time and working on the skill of listening has worked. I've recently realized I need to change the tapes in my head away from focusing on the loss my work-based connection. I do have a strong network of friends, an abundance of friendships — old and new, IRL and virtual, near and far. I have people in my life who give me energy, who are there if I need them, who I love spending time with, who I can talk to. I hope I can be the same for them.

Learning Moment: A Change of Plan

"The best-laid plans of mice and men". . . and apparently, retirement transitioners.

When life puts detours on your path, being resilient and adjusting is part of a successful retirement. And I am hell-bent on having a successful retirement.

What is the big detour in my path? I received a diagnosis of breast cancer.

First, let me shout – early detection!! Because of being conscientious in my screenings, my cancer is Stage 1. (Ladies – did you get your mammogram this year? Men – your prostate screening? Everyone who needs it – your colonoscopy?) So my prognosis is extremely positive. . . it's just a matter of being strong through the treatment.

So what changed on the retirement life plan? A bunch of half-made travel plans -- canceled. The plans for new holiday traditions and an open house from the move – went to the sidelines. Even my regular Fun with Friends planning -- all stopped. I had just gotten into the mindset of accepting that being the planner more-often-than-not was okay – it's a gift I'm giving to the others in the activities. But, plans have a way of going to the wayside when priorities shift to self-preservation.

What has not changed – continued focus on what is important and manageable during this time – self-care (how to keep up with yoga and walking, eating right, and being kind to myself), reading and writing (maybe time on my book editing, finally!), and even some light entertaining using that new kitchen. I will plan some quiet evenings – good friends will understand if I'm not at 100%, or barely 50% even!

I'm gonna be fine. I'm trying to stay with the positive attitude I learned to have in the past couple of years of retirement transition!

IN SUMMARY
Retirement is a Time for a New You

Retirement is an opportunity to unapologetically try new things, expand your horizons, or even just bask in the glow of what you have accomplished. It's the time to reinvent yourself, find the true you, and possibly try things you felt you missed out on.

For fifty-plus years, others dictated your life. Parents, school, bosses, family, and societal expectations controlled you and established your daily rhythm. You were expected to learn, achieve, and advance. And if you were like me, you tried really hard to meet expectations.

Societal expectations at this point include being a doting grandma, happy to be doing volunteer work, traveling as your heart desires, and maybe working part-time or actively engaged in your passion area. Well, I'm not a grandma (or a ma), am struggling with volunteering being meaningful, have had to acknowledge hubby is a homebody, and have yet to define a passion area. I wanted to. . . no I needed to, establish my own expectations.

Retirement is the time to move beyond societal expectations and establish your own! Focused on creating a new daily, almost ordinary, life pattern that is uniquely YOU!

- Clarify your values separate from societal expectations; understand when things are really just "shoulds" from others and when they are really your own desires.
- Come to terms with working (To work or not to work? What is right for you?). And volunteering (Is it a societal "should" or a true value?)
- Articulate your ideal retirement lifestyle. Curate your life activities to allow that vision to become a reality. Broaden your range of interests to find passion areas. Try on new things. Expand beyond your comfort zone just a bit.
- Invest in relationships.
- Build healthy living habits.
  - o Be physically active every day (or most days), including cardio, flexibility, and strengthening.
  - o Create healthy eating and sleeping habits.
  - o Practice positivity. Find joy in each day.
- Stop the Comparative Inferiority and the Negative Inner Voice. You are enough. You can. You will.
- Appreciate what you have. Have an attitude of gratitude.

Life is not a highlight reel. Retirement transition is finding a new personal, ordinary, daily rhythm that becomes second nature.

Your journey is unique – your circumstances, life experiences, values, interests, strengths all make it a unique path.

There is no magic bullet, no plug-it-in algorithm. You need to do the work yourself.

Know yourself. Create your vision. Start the journey.

Am I Done Transitioning?

At the writing of this book, I'm approaching the fourth anniversary of my retirement date (where did the time fly?). I started things that aligned with my retirement lifestyle vision based on my values, strengths, and interests. Because I love words, I've named them things like Couple Camaraderie, Walk & Talks, and Foodie Friends. I am trying to stop the bad behaviors (Waiting for Someday, Comparative Inferiority, food as a solution for boredom) and begin new habits (daily movement). I recognized losses of the old and continue to work on replacing the things I need, like identity and structure. I am finding that transitions can also threaten, as you give up old ways of doing things to take on new ways.

Am I done with the transition? No. My 21st Century Retirement Lifestyle is still a work in progress. I've discovered that (retirement) life is a series of transitions. I am still learning to be true to myself (versus others' expectations), trying new things, revising the plans with weekly calendars of activities. And I try to remember the journey is more important than the destination.

Enjoy the journey.

Top Ten Final Thoughts

I love top ten lists and avidly read ones others have posted. So here are the top ten things I've learned (so far) in post-work life and the world of blogging.

1. Have a life vision based on what's important to you. Own your choices of where you spend your time, so you're moving in the direction of your life vision. Stop listening to everyone else's "you really should." Keep refining that vision as you learn new things about what works for you and what doesn't.

2. Don't let fear drive procrastination. Take action; do something (something small, if needed). What are you waiting for? As Nike so aptly puts it: Just Do It. And celebrate those small advancements.

3. Have an attitude of gratitude – make gratitude lists regularly. Appreciate the activities you engage in, the people you interact with, the life you have created. Choose to be happy today. It's not something you have to earn in the future.

4. Proactive positivity. Use your tools to stay emotionally positive. No one embarks on a path not taken before and knows all the challenges that lie ahead. Life happens. But through it all, choose positive, proactive, affirming articulations. I am. I can. I will.

5. Be OK with being a beginner. Try new things. Take the opportunity when presented – say "yes." Give things a fair shot as

well; don't expect to be an expert immediately. If you like it, keep doing it. And be okay with less than perfection.. . . to dance and sing and write and draw and learn and explore.

6. Stop listening to the voice of Comparative Inferiority. Stop feeling guilty/unworthy/less if you're doing life differently. It's your unique life, your unique retirement. (Besides, you never see anyone else's complete life, you just see their highlight reel.)

7. Learn to just be sometimes. Let go of busyness as a sign of worth. It's not always about constant activity and checklists. And don't feel guilty that it is "wasted time."

8. Nurture your relationships. Be intentional in building connections, both physical and virtual, to ward off feelings of isolation. Appreciate the connections you do have – both IRL and virtual.

9. Move every day. Do something to get off the couch. And that doesn't mean just walk to the fridge.

10. Enjoy the journey. Savor life's little joys. Enjoy being in the moment.

APPENDIX

MY FAVORITES BOOK LIST FOR RETIREMENT TRANSITION

Don't Retire, Rewire by Jeri Sedlar and Rick Miners – A how-to on defining satisfaction drivers, separating skills and strengths, working through what in your work life was satisfied by your drivers. Introduces the interesting concept of four types of work: work for a wage, work for a fee, work for free, work for me.

The Joy of Retirement by David C. Borchard - Lots of how-to for defining who you want to be in retirement and the lifestyle that will help you be that person. Big sections on roles, talents, and values in defining your vision statement. Love the fact he does not assume where you will be on the continuum of working versus traditional leisure-based retirement.

How to Retire Happy, Wild and Free by Ernie J Zelinski – An easy-to-read conversational style. Introduces the possibilities "get a life tree." Real people case studies (as opposed to all professional, CEO types). The key difference here is a complete focus on "leisure" (not work).

The Artist's Way or ***The Artist's Way for Retirement*** by Julia Cameron. The original has a stronger introduction to her tools (Morning Pages, Artist Dates) but uses mostly art-based people as examples (filmmakers, musicians, writers, etc.). The focus is rekindling the artist within. The retirement version is more recent, uses retirees as examples, and has a core framework of your life memoir to help identify what interest/passion you might have "put to the side."

Your Retirement Quest by Alan Spector and Keith Lawrence – a good foundational book, focused on pre-retirement timing, but still covers all the bases; more of a case study approach.

65 Things to do When you Retire is in fact sixty-five interesting essays about retirement from all kinds of people, on all kinds of topics, many *very inspiring*. Edited by Mark Evans Chimsky

What Color is your Parachute - for Retirement by John E. Nelson and Richard N. Bolles - Some stuff on finances, but lots on health and happiness with great background on core values, theory and application of happiness (positive psychology), and practical how-to on self-reflection and life portfolio.

Now What? Know who you are, Get what you want by Laura Berman Fortgang. - Easy style, how-to-process with a focus on the second career or what did you always want to do so you will be happy. Good, insightful questions.

Second Act Careers by Nancy Collamer. – An in-depth look at part-time income stream possibilities with lots of resource connections.

The Couples Retirement Puzzle by Roberta K. Taylor and Dorian Mintzer. Unique in that it talks about *transitioning as a duo in life*. Covers all the big domains.

ABOUT THE AUTHOR

From Robert Frost: *two paths diverged in a wood,*
and I took the one less traveled.. . .

In July 2014, I retired from a thirty-plus-year corporate career in R&D with one Global Mega-Company. This timing was a few years earlier than planned, as a highly attractive, early retirement package was offered. Given the timing and my work-focused lifestyle, I did not have a plan in place for what came next. I am a planner by nature, so the days after the retirement moment became devoted to planning my journey of transition. I searched widely for how to figure it all out.

Part of the transition was (re)discovering who I wanted to be and what I wanted to do. I uncovered a desire to write, a love of research and synthesis, and a realization that I liked to advise/teach others. This all merged into the creation of this. . . a Retirement Transition book.

My focus is less about the money and more about the "Who am I now?" "What do I do with my time?" and "How do I figure this all out?"

I currently live in the Midwest (Cincinnati), with my also recently retired husband and our Lab-mix dog, Taylor. We all travel regularly to the Gulf Coast of Florida, where hubby would like to live permanently.

I blog about my continued journey at www.retirementtransition.blog

CPSIA information can be obtained
at www.ICGtesting.com
Printed in the USA
FFHW021233170319
51104944-56545FF